Hacking Vim 7.2

Ready-to-use hacks with solutions for common situations encountered by users of the Vim editor

Kim Schulz

PUBLISHING

BIRMINGHAM - MUMBAI

Hacking Vim 7.2

First published: April 2010

Production Reference: 1230410

Published by Packt Publishing Ltd.
32 Lincoln Road
Olton
Birmingham, B27 6PA, UK.

ISBN 978-1-849510-50-9

www.packtpub.com

Cover Image by Asher Wishkerman (a.wishkerman@mpic.de)

Credits

Author
Kim Schulz

Reviewers
Boris Fersing

Thomas Moyer

Development Editors
Darshana D. Shinde

Amey Kanse

Technical Editors
Madhumita Singh

Conrad Sardinha

Copy Editor
Sneha Kulkarni

Indexer
Hemangini Bari

Editorial Team Leader
Mithun Sehgal

Project Team Leader
Lata Basantani

Project Coordinator
Shubhanjan Chatterjee

Proofreader
Lynda Silwoski

Production Coordinator
Adline Swetha Jesuthas

Cover Work
Adline Swetha Jesuthas

About the Author

Kim Schulz has an M.Sc. in Software Engineering from Aalborg University in Denmark. He has been an active developer in the Linux and open source communities since 1997, and has worked with everything from translation and bug fixing to producing a full-blown software system.

Throughout this entire time, Vim has been Kim's "weapon" of choice and it is the first program he installs whenever he sits by a new computer.

Today Kim works as a Software engineer at CSR Plc, developing software for the next generation mobile and wireless technologies.

Kim is also the owner of a web hosting and development company, Devteam Denmark, that specializes in hosting of websites developed using the Fundanemt Content Management System—a CMS that Kim is a co-developer of.

I would like to thank my wife, Line, for letting me take the time to write this book. Without her positive attitude and help, I would never have gotten this book ready.

I would also like to add a great thank you to Bram Moolenaar for developing the Vim Editor—I appreciate the fruits of your work every day.

About the Reviewers

Boris Fersing is an amateur photographer and student in computational linguistics at the University of Saarland, Germany. For his studies, he participated in many projects and used many programming languages (SML, C/C++, Java, Ruby, Prolog) and Vim was always his editor of choice.

He also worked as system administrator for a department of the University of Saarland. With this job he learned how to use some Unix tools and improved his knowledge about the Vim editor.

> I really would like to thank the author for writing such a nice book. It was a pleasure to review it. The information it contains is really interesting. I recommend this book to everyone who wants to learn more about Vim.

Thomas Moyer is a graduate student in Computer Science and Engineering at Pennsylvania State University. He is currently looking at areas of Computer Security including trusted computing hardware and Web 2.0 security. He spends a great deal of time using Vim for editing both code and also writing papers. He has completed a Master's degree from Penn State and is currently working on his Ph.D.

> I would like to thank my wife and daughter for all of their support, and also the rest of my family. I would also like to thank the members of the Systems and Internet Infrastructure Security Lab at Penn State for their continued support.

Table of Contents

Preface

Back in the early days of the computer revolution, system resources were limited and developers had to figure out new ways to optimize their applications. This was also the case with the text editors of that time. One of the most popular editors of that time was an editor called Vim. It was optimized to near-perfection for the limited system resources on which it ran.

The world has come a long way since then, and even though the system resources have grown, many still stick with the Vim editor.

At first sight, the Vim editor might not look like much. However, if you look beneath the simple user interface, you will discover why this editor is still the favorite editor for so many people even today!

This editor has nearly every feature you would ever want, and if it's not in the editor, it is possible to add it by creating plugins and scripts. This high level of flexibility makes it ideal for many purposes, and is also one of the reasons why Vim is still one of the most advanced editors.

Many new users join the Vim user community everyday and want to use this editor in their daily work. And even though Vim can sometimes be complex to use, they still favor it above other editors. This is a book for these Vim users.

With this book, Vim users can make their daily work in the editor more comfortable and thereby optimize their productivity. In this way, they will not only have an optimized editor, but also an optimized workflow. The book will help them move from just using Vim as a simple text editor to a situation where they feel at home and can use it for many of their daily tasks.

Good luck and happy reading!

What this book covers

Chapter 1, Getting Started With Vim, introduces Vim and a few well-known relatives; their history and relation to vi is briefly described.

Chapter 2, Personalizing Vim, introduces how to make Vim a better editor for you by modifying it for your personal needs. It shows ways of modifying fonts, the color scheme, the status line, menus, and toolbar.

Chapter 3, Better Navigation, introduces some of the ways in which Vim helps us to navigate through files easily. It explains an alternative way for boosting navigation through files and buffers in Vim.

Chapter 4, Production Boosters, introduces you to features in Vim. It describes how to use templates, autocompletion, folding, sessions, and working with registers.

Chapter 5, Advanced Formatting, introduces simple tricks to format text and code. It also discusses how external tools can be used to give Vim just that extra edge it needs to be the perfect editor.

Chapter 6, Basic Vim Scripting, is especially for those who want to learn how to extend Vim with scripts. The chapter introduces scripting basic, and helps you write your first script.

Chapter 7, Extended Vim Scripting, takes off where Chapter 6 left the scripting by giving tips about how to write better scripts. An introduction to using external scripting languages will also be given in this chapter.

Appendix A, Vim Can Do Everything, has a listing of games that have been implemented with Vim scripting; it also provides an overview of chat and mail scripts and has a section on using Vim as an IDE.

Appendix B, Vim Configuration Alternatives, shows how to keep your Vim configuration files well-organized and retain your Vim configuration across computers by storing a copy of it online.

What you need for this book

Over the course of the last decade, Vim has evolved into a feature-rich editor. This means that some of the features from the later versions of Vim are not accessible in the older versions of Vim.

Vim is available for a wide variety of platforms and not all recipes will work on all platforms. This is typically due to the use of system-specific functionality that is not available on other platforms.

This book will focus on two of the platforms where Vim is most widespread, namely Linux and Microsoft Windows. As the Linux system resembles the system used in most Unix platforms, the recipes will work on other *NIX platforms.

 You can find the latest source code and binary packages for the Vim Editor at www.vim.org. If you use Linux it is, however, most likely that Vim is already packed with your Linux distribution as it is the default editor on most Linux systems.

Who this book is for

If you are a Vim user who wants to get more out of this legendary text editor, this book is for you. It focuses on making life easier for the intermediate to experienced Vim users.

New to Vim?

Even though this book is written assuming that the reader is already be familiar with Vim basics, it can still be used by newcomers to Vim.

If you are unsure about your extent of knowledge about Vim in order to continue reading this book, then I would recommend that you try out the Vimtutor that is included with your Vim installation.

Simply execute the Vimtutor program (placed together with your Vim installation) on your computer and it will then guide you through a range of practical lessons that teach you the Vim basics. Expect that it will take around 30 minutes to complete the entire Vimtutor tutorial.

The Vimtutor is available in many different languages. To use it in your language, you simply have to use the two-letter country code (such as ca, cs, de, el, eo, es, fr, hr, hu, it, ja, no, ro, and zh) as an argument to the Vimtutor program. For example, for the German version, you would use "vimtutor de".

Conventions

In this book, you will find a number of styles of text that distinguish between different kinds of information. Here are some examples of these styles, and an explanation of their meaning.

Code words in text are shown as follows: "If you look in the Vim help system by typing `:help 'statusline'`, you will see that the status line can contain a wide variety of pieces of information."

A block of code is set as follows:

```
function! InfoGuiTooltip()
    "get window count
    let wincount = tabpagewinnr(tabpagenr(),'$')
    let bufferlist=''
    "get name of active buffers in windows
    for i in tabpagebuflist()
        let bufferlist .= '['.fnamemodify(bufname(i),':t').'] '
    endfor
    return bufname($).' windows: '.wincount.' ' .bufferlist ' '
endfunction
```

Any command-line input or output is written as follows:

```
:amenu icon=/path/to/icon/myicon.png ToolBar.Bufferlist :buffers<cr>
```

New terms and **important words** are shown in bold. Words that you see on the screen, in menus or dialog boxes for example, appear in the text like this: "This command looks for the word **Error** (marked with a ^) at the beginning of all lines".

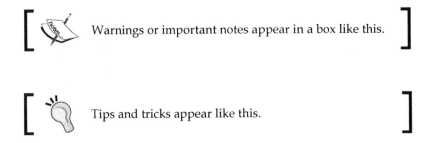

> Warnings or important notes appear in a box like this.

> Tips and tricks appear like this.

Reader feedback

Feedback from our readers is always welcome. Let us know what you think about this book—what you liked or may have disliked. Reader feedback is important for us to develop titles that you really get the most out of.

To send us general feedback, simply send an e-mail to feedback@packtpub.com, and mention the book title via the subject of your message.

If there is a book that you need and would like to see us publish, please send us a note in the **SUGGEST A TITLE** form on www.packtpub.com or e-mail suggest@packtpub.com.

If there is a topic that you have expertise in and you are interested in either writing or contributing to a book on, see our author guide on www.packtpub.com/authors.

Customer support

Now that you are the proud owner of a Packt book, we have a number of things to help you to get the most from your purchase.

Downloading the example code for the book

Visit http://www.packtpub.com/files/code/0509_Code.zip to directly download the example code.

The downloadable files contain instructions on how to use them.

Errata

Although we have taken every care to ensure the accuracy of our content, mistakes do happen. If you find a mistake in one of our books—maybe a mistake in the text or the code—we would be grateful if you would report this to us. By doing so, you can save other readers from frustration and help us improve subsequent versions of this book. If you find any errata, please report them by visiting http://www.packtpub.com/support, selecting your book, clicking on the **let us know** link, and entering the details of your errata. Once your errata are verified, your submission will be accepted and the errata will be uploaded on our website, or added to any list of existing errata, under the Errata section of that title. Any existing errata can be viewed by selecting your title from http://www.packtpub.com/support.

Piracy

Piracy of copyright material on the Internet is an ongoing problem across all media. At Packt, we take the protection of our copyright and licenses very seriously. If you come across any illegal copies of our works, in any form, on the Internet, please provide us with the location address or website name immediately so that we can pursue a remedy.

Please contact us at copyright@packtpub.com with a link to the suspected pirated material.

We appreciate your help in protecting our authors, and our ability to bring you valuable content.

Questions

You can contact us at questions@packtpub.com if you are having a problem with any aspect of the book, and we will do our best to address it.

1
Getting Started with Vim

The **Vim editor** (or **Vi IMproved**) was first released by Bram Moolenaar in November 1991 as a clone of the Unix vi editor for the Amiga platform.

The first release of Vim for the Unix platform was out a year later, and it started to become an alternative to the vi editor right away.

The combination of a more liberal licensing model, and the fact that Vim started to become a superset of vi's functionality resulted in it becoming progressively more popular with the open source community. Soon more and more Linux distributions started adopting Vim as an alternative to vi. Even if the users thought they used vi (if they actually executed the vi command), they opened Vim (the vi command had simply been substituted with a link to the vim command, which has often led to the misunderstanding that vi and Vim are actually the same program).

During the late 90s, Vim took over where vi was lacking behind in the so-called editor war that existed between the vi editor and the Emacs editor. Bram implemented a lot of the missing features that the Emacs community used as arguments for why Emacs was better than vi / Vim, but he did it without ever neglecting the main focus areas that the vi editor had right from the beginning.

Today, Vim is a feature-rich, fully configurable editor, loved by many. It supports syntax-highlighting of more than 200 different programming languages, autocompletion for a fast growing number of languages, folding, undo / redo, multiple buffers / windows / tabs, and a lot of other features.

In this chapter, we will take a look at the following items:

- How to get and install the vim editor
- The vim family of editors
- The license that vim is released under
- Common terminology used throughout the book

So, let's get started with this book.

Getting Vim

You might already be familiar with the Vim editor and have used it for a long time. If, however, you haven't played around with Vim yet, this is the right time to get a copy and install it on your system.

You will always be able to get the latest version of the Vim editor from the project web page at:

```
http://www.vim.org
```

 This book primarily focuses on Vim version 7.2, but don't worry if you have an older version—you can always upgrade your installation if you find that you need it.

On computers running Microsoft Windows, you simply run the downloaded .exe file and it will then take you through the installation. After installation, a shortcut to gVim will be available in the start menu.

On computers running Linux, the installation depends on the Linux distribution you are using. Chances are that you already have Vim installed as it comes pre-installed on most distributions today. If it is not already installed, then refer to the distributions package manager (for example Aptitude in debian, urpmi in Mandriva, and Synaptics in Ubuntu) to see how to install Vim. If no package manager is available, you can always install Vim from the source you downloaded using the previously mentioned link. See the readme file for information on the exact commands to use in order to install it.

vi, Vim, and friends

Vim is just one of many derivatives of the original vi that Bill Joy released back in 1976. Some have a feature list very close to that of vi, while others have chosen to add a wide variety of new features. Vim belongs to the group of vi clones that has chosen to add extra features. In the next section, we will introduce some of the better-known clones of vi and briefly describe the distinct features that each clone has.

vi

vi is the original root of the Vim family tree. It was created by Bill Joy in 1976 for one of the earlier versions of **Berkeley Software Distribution (BSD)**. The editor was an extension of the most common editor at that time, **ex**. Ex was, in turn, an extension of the Unix editor **ed**. The name "vi" is actually an abbreviation of **visual in ex**. As the name indicates, vi was actually just a command that started the ex editor in one of its modes—the visual mode.

vi was one of the first editors to introduce the concept of **modality**. What this means is that the editor has different modes for different tasks—one mode for editing text, another for selecting text, and yet another for executing commands.

This modality is one of the main features in vi, which makes enthusiasts like the editor, but it is also what makes others dislike it even more.

Not much has changed in vi since the first version, but it is still one of the most used editors in the Unix community. This is mainly because vi is considered a required application for Unix to comply with the **Single Unix Specification (SUS)**—and hereby be able to call itself a Unix.

STEVIE

In 1987, Tim Thompson got his first **Atari ST (Sixteen / Thirty-two)**. In this platform, there weren't any really good editors and so, he decided to clone the vi editor, which was known from the Unix platform. In June 1987, he released an editor under a license that resembles what has later become known as open source. He released it on Usenet and named it **STEVIE**—an abbreviation for **ST Editor for VI Enthusiasts**.

It was very simple and provided only a very small subset of the functionality that vi provided. It did, however, provide a familiar environment for vi users moving to the ST.

After the release, Tim Thompson discontinued work on the editor. But soon Tony Andrews took over, and within a year he had ported it to Unix and OS/2. More features were added along the way, but at some point around 1990, the development stopped.

STEVIE as an editor might not have survived throughout the years, but since both Tim and Tony released the source code on Usenet as public-domain for anyone to use, a lot of the later vi clones have been both inspired and based on this code.

Elvis

STEVIE was one of the more common editors around. It was, however, full of bugs and had some quite impractical limitations. Steve Kirkendall, who at that time used the operating system Minix, noticed one very big limitation, that is, the STEVIE editor held the entire file in memory while editing. This was not an optimal solution when using Minix, so Steve decided to rewrite the editor to use a file as buffer instead of editing in RAM. This turned into **Elvis**, version 1.0.

Even though Elvis was an improvement over the vi editor, it still suffered from some of the same limitations that vi had—maximum length of lines and only a single file buffer.

Steve Kirkendall decided to rewrite Elvis completely to get rid of the limitations, and this turned into Elvis version 2, which is the generation of the editor currently available (version 2.2).

With generation 2 of Elvis, Steve also included support for a range of other features that weren't in the original vi editor. Among these, a few features that are interesting and worth mentioning are:

- Syntax highlighting
- Multiple windows support
- Networking support (HTTP and FTP)
- Simple GUI frontends

Elvis is not actively developed anymore, but is still widely used. It is available for Unix, MS Windows (console or GUI with WinElvis), and OS/2.

 The latest version of the Elvis editor can always be found here at `http://elvis.the-little-red-haired-girl.org/`.

nvi

nvi, or **new vi** (as its full name is), is a result of a license dispute between AT&T and the **Computer Science Research Group** (**CSRG**) at University of California, Berkeley. vi was based on an original code from the ed editor, which was under the AT&T System V Unix license, so it was not possible for CSRG to distribute vi with BSD.

CSRG decided to replace the vi editor with an alternative editor under a freer license—their own BSD license.

Keith Bostic was the man that took on the job to make the new vi. The vi clone Elvis was already freely available, but Keith wanted an editor that resembled the original vi editor even more. He took the code for Elvis and transformed it into an almost 100 percent vi compatible clone—the nvi editor. Only the **Open Mode** and the **lisp edit** option from the original vi functionality set is left out.

By the release of 4.4BSD, the vi editor was completely substituted by nvi, and the software distribution was once again completely covered by a free license.

Today nvi is the default vi editor in most BSD-derived distributions such as NetBSD, FreeBSD, and OpenBSD, and has evolved into a more feature-rich editor than the original vi.

Compared to the original vi editor, nvi has been extended to support new features such as:

- Multiple edit buffers
- Unlimited undo
- Extended regular expressions
- CScope support
- Primitive scripting support in Perl and Tcl / Tk

Keith Bostic is still the maintainer of the nvi source code, but not much development has been done to the code for some time now.

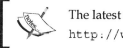 The latest version of the nvi editor can always be found here at http://www.bostic.com/vi/.

Vim

The **Vim** editor is the golden child of the vi family. Ever since Bram Moolenaar released the first version of Vim to the public in November 1991, this editor has evolved into one of the most feature-rich editors around.

The first version of Vim was, like the Elvis editor, based on the source code of the STEVIE editor. Bram, however, released Vim only for the Amiga platform, which was one of the most widespread platforms, at that time, among home computer enthusiasts. At that time Vim was an abbreviation for **Vi IMitation**, which described Vim quite well, in that it simply tried to do what vi did.

However, a year later in 1992, Bram made a port of his Vim editor for the Unix platform. The result of this was that Vim went beyond simply being a clone of vi for a different platform, to becoming a competitor. The development of Vim was quick and fast, and soon Vim had a range of features that the original vi editor did not have. Because of this, the abbreviation Vim was at some point changed into being Vi IMproved instead of Vi IMitation.

Within a couple of years, Vim grew to having a range of features that a lot of vi users missed. This made more and more users switch over to using Vim instead of vi as their primary editor.

In 1998, the fifth generation of Vim was released, and with it one of the most used features of today, scripting, was introduced.

Now, it was possible for the user to write their own scripts for Vim, and in that way expand the functionality of the editor. This was a really strong addition to the feature set of Vim because it would normally have required coding in a lower-level language, and recompilation of the editor in order to add even simple features.

A lot of features have been added to Vim throughout the last decade, and many of these are quite unique compared to the other editors and vi clones in particular.

Here, we will list just a few of the more distinct features of Vim, as the complete feature list would be too long:

- Editing multiple files in multiple buffers, windows, and tabs
- Advanced scripting language
- Support for scripting in Perl and Python
- Syntax highlighting for more than 200 programming languages
- Unlimited undo / redo with branching
- Context-aware completion of words and functions
- Advanced pattern-matching with regular expressions
- Close integration with a wide range of compilers, interpreters, and debuggers
- More than 1500 Vim scripts freely available online

Vim is available for an enormous variety of platforms such as all types of Unix, Linux, MS Dos, MS Windows, AmigaOS, Atari MiNT, OS/2, OS/390, MacOS, OpenVMS, RISC OS, and QNX.

Vile

Vile maybe the vi clone that looks least like the original vi editor — some would even say that it's not a clone at all. Vile is actually an attempt to bring the best of two worlds together in one editor — the modality of vi and the feature set of Emacs.

This also explains the name Vile, which is the shortform for **VI Like Emacs**.

The Vile editor project was started by Paul Fox during the summer of 1990. The code was based on the core code from the public-domain editor, **MicroEmacs**. Paul then modified it to have modality and other vi-like features.

The MicroEmacs code did not have all the features of the Emacs editor, but it had support for long lines and editing multiple files in multiple windows at the same time. These were features that vi did not have and which many programmers needed in their editor.

A lot of work was done to get the MicroEmacs code to be more vi-like, and several other developers joined the project. Thomas E. Dickey joined the project in 1992 and added a wide variety of features to Vile and fixed a lot of bugs in the code.

In 1994, Kevin Buettner joined the project and started working on the GUI version of vile — **xvile**. He added support for some of the most common widget sets at that time, such as Athena, OpenLook, Motif, and the Xt Toolkit.

Today, Thomas is the primary maintainer of Vile and the development is steered by him. His time for working on the editor is, however, very limited. So, it is mostly only bugfixes that he adds to the editor.

Vi and Vile are not very similar in the way they work, and only a minor subset of the vi features are present in Vile. The main features of Vile are:

- Editing modes — one mode for each file type
- Vile procedure language for macros
- (Experimental) Perl support
- Named functions that can be bound to keys as the user wishes

Vile is available for Unix, Linux, BeOS, OS/2, VMS, and MS Windows and exists in both a console version and a GUI version.

The latest version of the vile editor can always be found here at
`http://invisible-island.net/vile/vile.html`.

Compatibility

Though all the vi clones have at some point tried to behave like the vi editor, most of them have evolved in very different directions. This means, even though a lot of them support features such as syntax highlighting, they do not necessarily implement them in the same way. Therefore, a syntax file from Vim cannot be used in Elvis.

Even the features that originate from vi are not necessarily implemented the same way. Some of the clones have implemented features less accurately than others. Maybe the idea behind the feature is the same, but the actual result of using it is completely different.

In the following table, I have tried to give a percentage of how accurately the mentioned clones resemble the vi editor (0 percent being least compatible and 100 percent being completely compatible). The comparison has been done by looking at how much effort the clone developers have made in order to implement the features of vi as precisely as possible.

Clone	vi compatibility	Comment
STEVIE	10%	Only a very small feature set in common.
Vile	10%	Only general concepts such as modes in common.
Elvis	80%	Large feature set in common, some features behave quite differently though.
Nvi	95%	Nearly perfect compatibility, but a range of the features behave differently.
Vim	99%	In the "compatible mode", nearly all features are compatible.

In the table, only the features that the clones share with vi are considered. This means, even though, for example, Vim has a lot of features that vi does not have, it still resembles vi very precisely on the features that they share. Besides this, Vim implements nearly all of the features that vi has. Only some of the features that Bram Moolenaar considered as bugs in vi are implemented differently in Vim. Note that in order to make Vim 99 percent compatible with vi, you will have to set it into compatible mode with the command:

```
:set compatible
```

In Vim you can read more about vi and Vim differences with the command:
`:help vi-differences`

Another interesting observation is that even though STEVIE implemented a subset of the vi functionality very accurately, it did not implement enough of the vi features to be considered a close relative.

Vim is charityware

Bram Moolenaar, the developer of the Vim editor, has chosen to release Vim under a so called charityware license. What this means is that you can copy Vim as much as you like, but in exchange you are encouraged to make donations to a charity.

You can read more about the project if you open Vim and execute the command:

`:help uganda`

You can also get more information about how you can sponsor the Vim project if you go to the website `http://www.vim.org/sponsor/`.

As a Vim sponsor, you will get to vote for new features that should be implemented in Vim. So, besides supporting a good cause, you will also get some say on how Vim will evolve in the future.

Common terminology

Some words tend to have a different meaning depending on who you ask, hence, we have made a short list of some of the words here:

- **Hacker**: A technology interested person that likes to explore tech-related things and optimize them to fit his and others' needs.
- **Hacking**: The process a hacker goes through when exploring and optimizing his software or hardware. "Hacking Vim" would hence refer to the process of optimizing the Vim editor to fit the hacker's (user's) needs.
- **Script**: A textual program consisting of one or more lines of code that runs in an interpreter. A script can be written in many different programming languages, but will have to use one that matches the interpreter.
- **Interpreter**: A program that reads lines in a script and executes them one by one. An interpreter can be built into another program such as the Vim editor.

Summary

In this chapter, we introduced Vim and looked at what this book is about. Vim is just one of many clones of the old Unix vi editor, so, to get a broader view of the vi family tree, this chapter introduced some of the more well-known clones. Their history and relation to vi were briefly described and we learned that even though the vi clones at some point have tried to be like vi, they are not really compatible with each other.

We looked a bit at the concept of charityware, and how the author of the Vim editor uses that to raise money for children in need in Uganda. Finally, we took a look at some of the terminology used in this book and why the book is called "Hacking Vim".

You are now ready to go on with the next chapter and learn about how to personalize your Vim editor.

2
Personalizing Vim

If you tend to use your computer a lot for editing files, you soon realize that having a good editor is of paramount importance. A good editor will be your best friend and help you with your daily tasks. But what makes an editor good?

Looking at the different editors available, we see that developers try to make some of them the best by adding features they think the users need. Other editors have accepted that they are not the best and instead try to be the simplest, most user-friendly, or fastest-loading editor around.

With the Vim editor, no one decides what's best for you. Instead, you are given the opportunity to modify a large range of settings to make Vim fit your needs. This means, the power is in the hands of the user, rather than the hands of the developers of the editor.

Some settings have to do with the actual layout of Vim (for example, colors and menus), while others change areas that affect how we work with Vim such as the key bindings that map certain key combinations to specific tasks.

In this chapter, we will introduce a list of recipes that will help you personalize Vim in such a way that it becomes your personal favorite.

You will find recipes for the following personalization tasks:

- Changing the fonts
- Changing the color scheme
- Personal highlighting
- A more informative status line
- Toggle menu and toolbar
- Adding your own menu and toolbar buttons
- Work area personalization

Some of these tasks contain more than one recipe because there are different aspects for personalizing Vim for that particular task. It is you, the reader, who decides which recipes (or parts of it) you would like to read and use.

Before we start working with Vim, there are some things that you need to know about your Vim installation, such as where to find the configuration files.

Where are the configuration files?

When working with Vim, you need to know a range of different configuration files. The location of these files is dependent on where you have installed Vim and the operating system that you are using.

In general, there are three configuration files that you must know where to find:

*   vimrc
*   gvimrc
*   exrc

The vimrc file is the main configuration file for Vim. It exists in two versions — global and personal.

The global vimrc file is placed in the folder where all of your Vim system files are installed. You can find out the location of this folder by opening Vim and executing the following command in normal mode:

`:echo $VIM`

The examples could be:

*   Linux: /usr/share/vim/vimrc
*   Windows: c:\program files\vim\vimrc

The personal vimrc file is placed in your home directory. The location of the home directory is dependent on your operating system. Vim was originally meant for Unixes, so the personal vimrc file is set to be hidden by adding a dot as the first character in the filename. This normally hides files on Unix, but not on Microsoft Windows. Instead, the vimrc file is prepended with an underscore on these systems. So, examples would be:

*   Linux: /home/kim/.vimrc
*   Windows: c:\documents and settings\kim_vimrc

Whatever you change in the personal `vimrc` file will overrule any previous setting made in the global `vimrc` file. This way you can modify the entire configuration without having to ever have access to the global `vimrc` file.

You can find out what Vim considers as the home directory on your system by executing the following command in normal mode:

`:echo $HOME`

Another way of finding out exactly which `vimrc` file you use as your personal file is by executing the following command in the normal mode:

`:echo $MYVIMRC`

The `vimrc` file contains `ex` (vi predecessor) commands, one on each line, and is the default place to add modifications to the Vim setup. In the rest of the book, this file is just called `vimrc`.

Your `vimrc` can use other files as an external source for configurations. In the `vimrc` file, you use the `source` command like this:

`source /path/to/external/file`

Use this to keep the `vimrc` file clean, and your settings more structured. (Learn more about how to keep your `vimrc` clean in Appendix B, *Vim Configuration Alternatives*).

The `gvimrc` file is a configuration file specifically for Gvim. It resembles the `vimrc` file previously described, and is placed in the same location as a personal version as well as a global version. For example:

- Linux: `/home/kim/.gvimrc` and `/usr/share/vim/gvimrc`
- Windows: `c:\documents and settings\kim\_gvimrc` and `c:\program files\vim\gvimrc`

 This file is used for GUI-specific settings that only Gvim will be able to use. In the rest of the book, this file is called `gvimrc`.

The `gvimrc` file does not replace the `vimrc` file, but is simply used for configurations that only apply to the GUI version of Vim. In other words, there is no need to have your configurations duplicated in both the `vimrc` file and the `gvimrc` file.

The `exrc` file is a configuration file that is only used for backwards compatibility with the old vi / ex editor. It is placed at the same location (both global and local) as `vimrc`, and is used the same way. However, it is hardly used anymore except if you want to use Vim in a vi-compatible mode.

Changing the fonts

In regular Vim, there is not much to do when it comes to changing the font because the font follows one of the terminals. In Gvim, however, you are given the ability to change the font as much as you like.

The main command for changing the font in Linux is:

```
:set guifont=Courier\ 14
```

Here, `Courier` can be exchanged with the name of any font that you have, and 14 with any font size you like (size in points — pt).

For changing the font in Windows, use the following command:

```
:set guifont=Courier:14
```

If you are not sure about whether a particular font is available on the computer or not, you can add another font at the end of the command by adding a comma between the two fonts. For example:

```
:set guifont=Courier\ New\ 12, Arial\ 10
```

If the font name contains a whitespace or a comma, you will need to escape it with a backslash. For example:

```
:set guifont=Courier\ New\ 12
```

This command sets the font to Courier New size 12, but only for this session. If you want to have this font every time you edit a file, the same command has to be added to your `gvimrc` file (without the `:` in front of `set`).

 In Gvim on Windows, Linux (using GTK+), Mac OS, or Photon, you can get a font selection window shown if you use this command: `:set guifont=*`.

If you tend to use a lot of different fonts depending on what you are currently working with (code, text, logfiles, and so on.), you can set up Vim to use the correct font according to the file type. For example, if you want to set the font to Arial size 12 every time a normal text file (`.txt`) is opened, this can be achieved by adding the following line to your `vimrc` file:

```
autocmd BufEnter *.txt set guifont=Arial\ 12
```

The window of Gvim will resize itself every time the font is changed. This means, if you use a smaller font, you will also (as a default) have a smaller window. You will notice this right away if you add several different file type commands like the one previously mentioned, and then open some files of different types. Whenever you switch to a buffer with another file type, the font will change, and hence the window size too.

 You can find more information about changing fonts in the Vim help system under **Help | guifont**.

Changing color scheme

Often, when working in a console environment, you only have a black background and white text in the foreground. This is, however, both dull and dark to look at. Some colors would be desirable.

As a default, you have the same colors in the console Vim as in the console you opened it from. However, Vim has given its users the opportunity to change the colors it uses. This is mostly done with a color scheme file. These files are usually placed in a directory called `colors` wherever you have installed Vim.

You can easily change the installed color schemes with the command:

```
:colorscheme mycolors
```

Here, `mycolors` is the name of one of the installed color schemes. If you don't know the names of the installed color schemes, you can place the cursor after writing:

```
:colorscheme
```

Now, you can browse through the names by pressing the *Tab* key. When you find the color scheme you want, you can press the *Enter* key to apply it.

The color scheme not only applies to the foreground and background color, but also to the way code is highlighted, how errors are marked, and other visual markings in the text.

You will find that some color schemes are very alike and only minor things have changed. The reason for this is that the color schemes are user supplied. If some user did not like one of the color settings in a scheme, he or she could just change that single setting and re-release the color scheme under a different name.

Play around with the different color schemes and find the one you like. Now, test it in the situations where you would normally use it and see if you still like all the color settings. In Chapter 6, *Basic Vim Scripting*, we will get back to how you can change a color scheme to fit your needs perfectly.

```
/**
 * Main algorithm to keep processing while ther
 */
private void run() {
    // Only invoke this once even though we recei
    if (running) {
        System.out.println("Client is already runni
        return;
    } else
        running = true;

    // Only do actual work if there any workunits
    while (currentWorkUnit != null) {
        System.out.println("Acquiring workunits");
        if (!queueWorkunits())
            continue;
        System.out.println("Queueing threads for ex
        queueWorkers();
        System.out.println("Awaiting results from
        commitResults()
    }
    System.out.println("Ending connection with se
}
```

Personal highlighting

In Vim, the feature of highlighting things is called **matching**.

With matching, you can make Vim mark almost any combination of letters, words, numbers, sentences, and lines. You can even select how it should be marked (errors in red, important words in green, and so on).

Matching is done with the following command:

```
:match Group /pattern/
```

The command has two arguments. The first one is the name of the color group that you will use in the highlight.

Compared to a color scheme, which affects the entire color setup, a color group is a rather small combination of background (or foreground) colors that you can use for things such as matches. When Vim is started, a wide range of color groups are set to default colors, depending on the color scheme you have selected.

To see a complete list of color groups, use the command:

```
:so $VIMRUNTIME/syntax/hitest.vim.
```

The second argument is the actual pattern you want to match. This pattern is a regular expression and can vary from being very simple to extremely complex, depending on what you want to match. A simple example of the match command in use would be:

```
:match ErrorMsg /^Error/
```

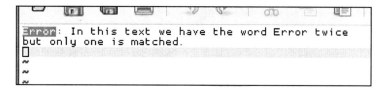

This command looks for the word **Error** (marked with a ^) at the beginning of all lines. If a match is found, it will be marked with the colors in the `ErrorMsg` color group (typically white text on red background).

If you don't like any of the available color groups, you can always define your own. The command to do this is as follows:

```
:highlight MyGroup ctermbg=red guibg=red gctermfg=yellow
    guifg=yellow term=bold
```

This command creates a color group called `MyGroup` with a red background and yellow text, in both the console (Vim) and the GUI (Gvim). You can change the following options according to your preferences:

cformb	Background color in console
guibg	Background color in Gvim
ctermf	Text color in console
guifg	Text color in Gvim
gui	Font formatting in Gvim
term	Font formatting in console (for example, bold)

If you use the name of an existing color group, you will alter that group for the rest of the session.

When using the match command, the given pattern will be matched until you perform a new match or execute the following command:

```
:match NONE
```

The match command can only match one pattern at a time, so Vim has provided you with two extra commands to match up to three patterns at a time. The commands are easy to remember because their names resemble those of the match command:

`:2match`

`:3match`

You might wonder what all this matching is good for, as it can often seem quite useless. Here are a few examples to show the strength of matching.

Example 1: Mark color characters after a certain column

In mails, it is a common rule that you do not write lines more than 74 characters (a rule that also applies to some older programming languages such as, Fortran-77). In a case like this, it would be nice if Vim could warn you when you reached this specific number of characters.

This can simply be done with the following command:

`:match ErrorMsg /\%>73v.\+/`

Here, every character after the 73rd character will be marked as an error. This match is a regular expression that when broken down consists of:

\%>	Match after column with the number right after this
73	The column number
V	Tells that it should work on virtual columns only
.\+	Match one or more of any character

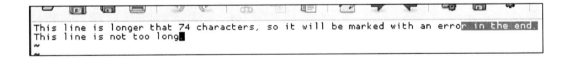

```
This line is longer that 74 characters, so it will be marked with an error in the end.
This line is not too long
~
```

Example 2: Mark tabs not used for indentation in code

When coding, it is generally a good rule of thumb to use tabs only to indent code, and not anywhere else. However, for some it can be hard to obey this rule. Now, with the help of a simple match command, this can easily be prevented.

The following command will mark any tabs that are not at the beginning of the line (indentation) as an error:

```
:match errorMsg /[^\t]\zs\t\+/
```

Now, you can check if you have forgotten the rule and used the *Tab* key inside the code. Broken down, the match consists of the following parts:

[^	Begin a group of characters that should not be matched
\t	The tab character
]	End of the character group
\zs	A zero-width match that places the "matching" at the beginning of the line, ignoring any whitespaces
\t\+	One or more tabs in a row

```
int Main(int count{
    int number = 4;            //some number
    float digit = 2.3f;        //some diget
}
```

This command says: Don't match all the tab characters; match only the ones that are not used at the beginning of the line (ignoring any whitespaces around it).

If instead of using tabs you want to use the space character for indentation, you can change the command to:

```
:match errorMsg /[\t]/
```

This command just says: Match all the tab characters.

Example 3: Preventing errors caused by IP addresses

If you write a lot of IP addresses in your text, sometimes you tend to enter a wrong value in one (such as 123.123.123.256). To prevent this kind of an error, you can add the following match to your `vimrc` file:

```
match errorMsg /\(2[5][6-9]\|2[6-9][0-9]\|[3-9][0-9][0-9]\)[.]
            \[0-9]\{1,3\}[.][0-9]\{1,3\}[.][0-9]\{1,3\}\|
            \[0-9]\{1,3\}[.]\(2[5][6-9]\|2[6-9][0-9]\|\
            \\ \[3-9][0-9][0-9]\)[.][0-9]\{1,3\}[.][0-9]
            \\{1,3\}\|\[0-9]\{1,3\}[.][0-9]\{1,3\}[.]\(2[5]
            \\ \[6-9]\|\2[6-9][0-9]|[3-9][0-9][0-9]\)[.]
            [0-9]\{1,3\}
            \\|[0-9]\{1,3\}[.][0-9]\{1,3\}[.][0-9]\{1,3\}[.]
            \\(2[5][6-9]\|2[6-9][0-9]\|\[3-9][0-9][0-9]\)/
```

Even though this seems a bit too complex for solving a small possible error, you have to remember that even if it helps you just once, it is worth adding.

> If you want to match valid IP addresses, you can use this, which is a much simpler command:
>
> ```
> match todo /\(\(25[0-5]\|2[0-4][0-9]\|[01]\?[0-9]
>                 [0-9]\?\)\.\)
>             \\ \{3\}\(25[0-5]\|2[0-4][0-9]\|[01]\?
>                 [0-9][0-9]\?\)/
> ```

A more informative status line

At the bottom of the Vim editor, you will find two things:

- The command line buffer (where you can input commands)
- The status line

In the default configuration, Vim has a simple and quite non-informative status line. To the right it shows the number of the current row and column, and to the left it shows the name of the file currently open (if any).

Whenever you execute a Vim command, the status line will disappear and the command buffer will be shown in that line instead. If the command you execute writes any messages, then those will be shown on the right of the status line.

For simple and fast file editing, this status line is adequate. But if you use Vim everyday and for a lot of different file formats, it would be nice to have a more informative status line.

In this recipe, we see some examples of how the status line can be made a lot more informative with simple methods.

The command that sets how the status line should look is simply called:

```
:set statusline format
```

Here, `format` is a **string** such as `printf` (known from C programming) that describes how the status line should look.

If you look in the Vim help system by typing `:help 'statusline'`, you will see that the status line can contain a wide variety of pieces of information. Some of these are more useful in your daily work than others.

My status line always contains information about:

- Name of the file that I am editing
- Format of the file that I am editing (DOS, Unix)
- File type as recognized by Vim for the current file
- ASCII and hex value of the character under the cursor
- Position in the document as row and column number
- Length of the file (line count)

The following command will turn your status line into a true information bar with all the previously mentioned information:

```
:set statusline=%F%m%r%h%w\ [FORMAT=%{&ff}]\ [TYPE=%Y]\ [ASCII=\%03.3b]\
[HEX=\%02.2B]\ [POS=%04l,%04v]\ [%p%%]\ [LEN=%L]
```

I have added a `[ ]` around each of the pieces of information so that it is easier to distinguish them from each other. This is purely to give a visual effect and can be left out if necessary.

However, we now see that the status line still shows the old non-informative status line, as in the default installation. This problem occurs because Vim, by default, does not show the status line at all. Instead, it just shows the command buffer with a little bit of information in it. To tell Vim that you would like to have a real status line shown, you will have to add the following setting to your `vimrc` file. This command will make sure that your status line is always shown as the second-last line in the editor window:

```
:set laststatus=2
```

You will now see that the command buffer gets a place of its own in the last line of the editor window. This way there's always room for the status line and you will always have information about the file right in front of you. The status line does, of course, take up some of the editing area, but it is then up to you to decide whether it should be shown or not. You can always remove it for the rest of the editing session by executing the following command from within Vim:

```
:set laststatus=0
```

Toggle menu and toolbar

If you are used to working with Vim in the console mode, you are also quite used to having no menus and toolbars at the top of the window. However, when you move to Gvim, you will soon realize that both the menu and the toolbar are present by default in the GUI.

Many believe that extra room for text is far more important than the menu and the toolbar. If you are one of those persons, you might like to remove the menu and toolbar while working in Gvim. However, some scripts add useful functionality in the menu and it is, therefore, important to have menus. The solution for this could be toggling if the menu and toolbar are shown or not.

The following code maps the key combination *Ctrl+F2* to toggle the menu and toolbar in Gvim. You can add it to your `vimrc` file if you want this functionality.

```
map <silent> <C-F2> :if &guioptions =~# 'T' <Bar>
                \set guioptions-=T <Bar>
                \set guioptions-=m <bar>
        \else <Bar>
                \set guioptions+=T <Bar>
                \set guioptions+=m <Bar>
            \endif<CR>
```

Now, whenever you don't need the menu and toolbar, you can just press *Ctrl+F2* and you will get the full space for your text.

If you want either the menu or the toolbar to be hidden all the time, add one of the following lines to your `vimrc` file.

To remove the menu completely, add:

```
:set guioptions-=m
```

To remove the toolbar completely, add:

```
:set guioptions-=T
```

> Other parts of the GUI can be modified with the `set guioptions` command. To find out what you can modify, look in `:help 'guioptions'`.

Adding your own menu and toolbar buttons

If you are in Gvim, you can make a handy menu with all the functionality you use the most. You might not always need to use it from the menu, but whenever you forget how to use it, you can always just find it there. If you need to get to the functionality really fast, you can even add it directly in the toolbar of Gvim.

In this recipe, we look at both how to make your own menu and, later, how to add extra buttons to the toolbar in Gvim. Let's start with the menu construction.

Adding a menu

Building a menu is basically just executing a command for each item you want in the menu. As long as you follow the right naming convention, you will see a nice little menu with all your items in it.

Let's start with a simple example. Say you want to add a menu like the buffers menu, but for tabs.

The command you will need to use is:

`:menu menupath command`

This command works much like the `map` command, except that instead of mapping a command to a key combination, here the mapping is done to a menu item.

The command has two arguments. The first is the actual path in the menu where the item should be placed, and the second argument is the command that the menu item should execute. If, for instance, you want to add a menu item called **Next** to the menu item **Tabs**, then you would need to use a command like this:

`:menu Tabs.Next <ESC>:tabnext<cr>`

So, now you have a menu called **Tabs** with one menu item called **Next**. Now, the **Next** menu item executes the following command:

`:tabnext`

This command is prepended with `<ESC>` to get into the normal mode, and then `<cr>` to actually execute the command. If you haven't added `<ESC>`, this command won't work. Another way to get around this is by adding specific menu items according to the current mode. For this, Vim has a range of alternatives to the `:menu` command:

- `:nmenu` for the **Normal** mode
- `:imenu` for the **Insert** mode, `^o` is prepended
- `:vmenu` for the **Visual** mode, `^c` is prepended and `^\^G` is appended
- `:cmenu` for the **Command-line** mode, `^c` is prepended and `^\^G` is appended
- `:omenu` for the **OP-pending** mode, `^c` is prepended and `^\^G` is appended

The prepended parts (^o and ^c) are to get into normal mode.

The ^o (*Ctrl + O*) is especially for insert mode because it gets you back into insert mode after executing the command.

^\^G (*Ctrl + \, Ctrl + G*) is to handle the special case wherein the global insert mode setting is set to true and Vim has the insert mode as the default mode (Vim is modeless). In this case, it will get you back into the insert mode and in the rest of the case, it will get you back in the mode you just came from.

> Instead of setting the same menu item for each and every mode, you can just replace the commands with this single command:
> `:amenu menu-path command`
>
> According to the current mode, this command prepends and appends things to the right.

So, let's go to our new **Tabs** menu, and add some more items and functionality to it. With the following, it should look similar to the **Buffers** menu:

```
:amenu Tabs.&Delete :confirm tabclose<cr>
:amenu Tabs.&Alternate          :confirm tabn #<cr>
:amenu <silent> Tabs.&Next      :tabnext<cr>
:amenu <silent>Tabs.&Previous   :tabprevious<cr>
```

The observant reader might have noticed that some new things have been added in the commands.

The first thing is the `<silent>` tag in the last two commands. By adding this, we can avoid the command being echoed in the command-line buffer during execution. Although, this is purely a cosmetic functionality, the `&` in the menu path is a more functional extension. By adding `&` in front of one of the letters in the last part of the menu path, you can define a keyboard shortcut for an item. This makes it easy to navigate to that particular item in the menu and execute it.

Let's say that you want to go to the next tab by executing the **Tabs | Next** menu item. Now, you can do so by simply pressing *Alt + T + N*. This is *Alt + T* for opening **Tabs**, and *N* (*N* because the & is in front of the N in Next) to call the **Next** item. If another menu item uses the same character for a shortcut, you can cycle through it by pressing the *Alt* key repeatedly.

If you would like to have a line that separates some of the items in your drop-down menu, you can use the name SEP for the item and ":" for the command:

`:amenu Tabs.-SEP-:`

The menu that we have created will only exist as long as Vim is open in this session. So, in order to get it into your menu all the time, you need to add it to your `vimrc` file (without the `:` in front of the commands).

So, now we have a simple **Tabs** menu that looks a bit like the **Buffers** menu. It does not, however, have the functionality that lists active buffers in the **Buffers** menu. This does not make much of a difference when you realize that buffers can be hidden for the user, but tabs cannot. You can, in other words, always see exactly how many tabs you have and what they are called by just looking at the tab bar.

A **Personal** menu can be used for a lot of other interesting things. If you work with many types of files, you can even start having menus for specific file types or submenus for the different types in the same menu.

A submenu is constructed by following the naming convention in the menu path. So, if you want to navigate through **Tabs | Navigation | Next**, you will simply have to add the **Next** menu item with the `Tabs.Navigation.&Next` menu path.

Adding toolbar icons

So, now that we know how to make our menus, adding our own icons to the toolbar isn't that difficult. Actually, Vim is constructed in such a way that the toolbar is just another menu with a special name. Hence, adding an icon to the toolbar is just like adding an item to a menu.

In the case of a toolbar menu, you will be able to add items to it by using a menu path that starts with the name `ToolBar`. To add an item to the toolbar that gives access for executing the `:buffers` command (show list of open buffers), all you have to do is to execute the following command:

`:amenu icon=/path/to/icon/myicon.png ToolBar.Bufferlist :buffers<cr>`

Of course, you will need to have an icon placed somewhere that can be shown in the toolbar.

The path to the icon is given with the `icon` argument to the `amenu` command. If you do not give a path to the file, but only the filename, then Vim will look for the icon in a folder called `bitmaps/` in the Vim runtime path (execute `:echo $VIMRUNTIME` to see where it is). The type of icons supported is dependent on the system you use it on.

And that's really it! After executing the command, you will see your icon in the toolbar as the last one on the right. If you press it, it will execute the `:buffers` command and show you a buffer list.

As with the menus, you can add toolbar buttons that are only shown in specific modes using the mode-specific menu commands `imenu`, `vmenu`, `cmenu`, and so on.

If you want your menu or toolbar icon placed elsewhere than to the right of the others, then you can use priorities. Read more about how you can do this in `:help menu-priority` and `:help sub-menu-priority`.

Modifying tabs

Ever since the release of Vim version 7.0, there has been support for tabs or tab pages as it is called. Tab pages are not like the normal tabs in other applications; rather they are a way to group your open files. Each tab can contain several open buffers and even several windows at the same time.

What makes tabs special is the commands that you would normally execute on all open buffers / windows (such as `:bufdo`, `:windo`, `:all`, and `:ball`) are limited to only the windows and buffers in the current tab page.

Normally, tab pages are shown as a list of tabs at the top of the window (just above the editing area). Each tab has a label, which by default shows the name of the file in the currently active buffer. If more windows are open at the same time in the tab page, then the tab label will also show a number telling how many windows.

Sometimes you might like to have the label on the tabs telling you something different. For instance, if you often have one tab for each project, then it would be nice to name the tab according to the name of the project in it.

The label on the tabs is set in a way very similar to the one used for the status line (see the *A more informative status line* section). But here, instead of setting the `status line` property, you set the `tabline` property:

```
:set tabline=tabline-layout
```

However, if you are in Gvim use the following line:

```
:set guitablabel
```

Even though setting the tabline resembles the way you set the status line, it is a bit more troublesome. This is mainly because you need to take care of whether the tab is an active one or not. So, let's start with a little example for Vim.

When we have a lot of tabs, they tend to take up too much space in the tab page, especially if they contain the entire name of the file in the currently active buffer. We want to have only the first six letters of the name of the active buffer in the tab label. The active tab should also be easy to distinguish from the other tabs. So, let's make its colors white on red like error messages.

The following script in Vim script does just that (learn more about how to create Vim scripts in Chapter 6).

```
function ShortTabLine()
  let ret = ''
  for i in range(tabpagenr('$'))
    " select the color group for highlighting active tab
    if i + 1 == tabpagenr()
    let ret .= '%#errorMsg#'
  else
    let ret .= '%#TabLine#'
  endif
        " find the buffername for the tablabel
    let buflist = tabpagebuflist(i+1)
    let winnr = tabpagewinnr(i+1)
    let buffername = bufname(buflist[winnr - 1])
    let filename = fnamemodify(buffername,':t')
  " check if there is no name
```

```
    if filename == ''
      let filename = 'noname'
    endif
    " only show the first 6 letters of the name  and
    " .. if the filename is more than 8 letters long
    if strlen(filename) >=8
        let ret .= '['. filename[0:5].'..]'
    else
        let ret .= '['.filename.']'
    endif
  endfor
  " after the last tab fill with TabLineFill and reset tab page #
  let ret .= '%#TabLineFill#%T'
  return ret
endfunction
```

Now, we have the function and just need to add it to our `vimrc` file, along with
a line that sets the tabline to the output of our function. This can be done with the
following command:

```
:set tabline=%!ShortTabLine()
```

The result is a more compact tablist as shown in the following screenshot:

Changing the tabline in Gvim is a bit different, but still follows almost the same basic
ideas. However, when in the GUI, you do not have to consider things such as the
color of the active tab, or whether it is actually active or not because this is all a part
of the GUI design itself.

So, let's simplify the `ShortTabLine()` function a bit so that it only sets the tab label:

```
function ShortTabLabel()
    let bufnrlist = tabpagebuflist(v:lnum)
    " show only the first 6 letters of the name + ..
    let label = bufname(bufnrlist[tabpagewinnr(v:lnum) - 1])
    let filename = fnamemodify(label,':h')
    " only add .. if string is more than 8 letters
    if strlen(filename) >=8
       let ret=filename[0:5].'..'
    else
      let ret = filename
    endif
        return ret
    endfunction
```

So, now we just have to set the `guitablabel` property to the output of our function:

```
:set guitablabel=%{ShortTabLabel()}
```

The result will be fine, small tabs as shown in the following figure.

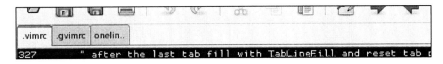

If you want to remove the tabs bar completely from Gvim, then you can use the:`:set showtabline=0` command (set to 1 to show it again).

Now we have limited the information in the tabs, but we would still like to have the information somewhere. For that we have a nice little tip—use the tool tips.

The nice thing about tool tips is that when you don't activate them (hold your cursor over some area, for example, a tab), you don't see them. This way you can have the information without it filling up the entire editor.

To set the tool tip for a tab, you will need to use the following command:

```
:set guitabtooltip
```

This property should be set to the value you want to show when the mouse cursor hovers over the tab.

To test it, you can try it with a simple execution like this:

```
:set guitabtooltip='my tooltip'
```

Now, this only shows a static text in the tool tip. We need some more information there. We removed the path from the filenames on the tabs, but sometimes it is actually nice to have this information available. With the tool tips, this is easily shown with the following command:

```
:set guitabtooltip=%!bufname($)
```

As with the tabs, the contents of the tool tip can be constructed by a function. Here, we have constructed a small function that shows all the information you would normally have in the tabs, but in a more organized way:

```
function! InfoGuiTooltip()
    "get window count
```

```
    let wincount = tabpagewinnr(tabpagenr(),'$')
    let bufferlist=''
    "get name of active buffers in windows
    for i in tabpagebuflist()
        let bufferlist .= '['.fnamemodify(bufname(i),':t').'] '
    endfor
    return bufname($).' windows: '.wincount.' ' .bufferlist ' '
endfunction
```

Use the code described previously like this:

```
:set guitabtooltip=%!InfoGuiTooltip()
```

In the following screenshot, you can see how the resulting tool tip will look in Gvim:

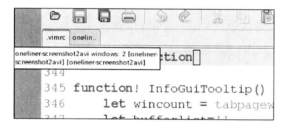

You can probably imagine many other interesting ways to use the small information space that the tabs and tool tips provide. Following the previous example, you should have no problems in implementing them.

Work area personalization

In this section, we introduce a list of smaller, good-to-know modifications for the editor area in Vim. The idea with these recipes is that they all give you some sort of help or optimization when you use Vim for editing text or code.

Adding a more visual cursor

Sometimes, you have a lot of syntax coloring in the file you are editing. This can make the task of tracking the cursor really hard. If you could just mark the line the cursor is currently in, then it would be easier to track it.

Many have tried to fix this with Vim scripts, but the results have been near useless (mainly due to slowness, which prevented scrolling longer texts at an acceptable speed). Not until version 7 did Vim have a solution for this. But then it came up with not just one, but two possible solutions for cursor tracking.

The first one is the `cursorline` command, which basically marks the entire line with, for example, another background color without breaking the syntax coloring. To turn it on, use the following command:

`:set cursorline`

The color it uses is the one defined in the `CursorLine` color group. You can change this to any color or styling you like, for example:

`:highlight CursorLine guibg=lightblue ctermbg=lightgray`

See the *Personal highlighting* section for more information on how to change a color group.

```
340          let ret = filename
341       endif
342         return ret
343       endfunction
344
345 function! InfoGuiTooltip()
346    let wincount = tabpagewinnr(tabpagenr(),'$')
347    let bufferlist=''
348    for i in tabpagebuflist()
349       let bufferlist .= '['.fnamemodify(bufname(i),':t').'] '
350    endfor
351    return bufname($).' windows: '.wincount.' '.bufferlist
352 endfunction
353 " check to see which changes you have made to the current buffer since last
354 " save.
355 function! DiffWithDiskFile()
```

If you are working with a lot of aligned file content (such as tab-separated data), the next solution for cursor tracking comes in handy:

`:set cursorcolumn`

This command marks the current column (here the cursor is placed) by coloring the entire column through the entire file, for example.

As with the cursor line, you can change the settings for how the cursor column should be marked. The color group to change is named `cursorcolumn`.

Adding both the cursor line and column marking makes the cursor look like a crosshair, thus making it impossible to miss.

```
340          let ret = filename
341       endif
342         return ret
343       endfunction
344
345 function! InfoGuiTooltip()
346    let wincount = tabpagewinnr(tabpagenr(),'$')
347    let bufferlist='
348    for i in tabpagebuflist()
349       let bufferlist .= '['.fnamemodify(bufname(i),':t').'] '
350    endfor
351    return bufname($).' windows: '.wincount.' '.bufferlist
352 endfunction
353 " check to see which changes you have made to the current buffer since last
354 " save.
355 function! DiffWithDiskFile()
```

Even though the `cursorline` and `cursorcolumn` functionalities are implemented natively in Vim, it can still give quite a slowdown when scrolling through the file.

Adding line numbers

Often when compiling and debugging code, you will get error messages stating that the error is in some line. One could, of course, start counting lines from the top to find the line, but Vim has a solution to go directly to some line number. Just execute :xxx where xxx is the line number, and you will be taken to the xxx line.

Alternatively, you can go into normal mode (press the *Esc* key) and then simply use xxxgg or xxxG (again xxx is the line number). Sometimes, however, it is nice to have an indication of the line number right there in the editor, and that's where the following command comes in handy:

`:set number`

Now, you get line numbers to the left of each line in the file. By default, the numbers take up four columns of space, three for numbers, and one for spacing. This means that the width of the numbers will be the same until you have more than 999 lines. If you get above this number of lines, an extra column will be added and the content will be moved to the right.

Of course, you can change the default number of columns used for the line numbers. This can be achieved by changing the following property:

`:set numberwidth=XXX`

Replace xxx with the number of columns that you want.

Even though it would be nice to make the number of columns higher in order to get more spacing between code and line numbers, this is not achievable with the `numberwidth` property. This is because the line numbers will be right-aligned within the columns.

In the following figure, you can see how line numbers are shown as right-aligned when a higher number of columns are set in `numberwidth`:

```
21    When we speak of free sof
22 price.  Our General Public
23 have the freedom to distri
24 this service if you wish),
25 if you want it, that you ca
26 in new free programs; and t
27
28    To protect your rights, w
29 anyone to deny you these ri
30 These restrictions translat
~/ontv/COPYING [FORMAT=unix] [TYPE=]
```

You can change the styling of the line numbers and the columns they are in by making changes to the `LineNr` color group.

Spell checking your language

We all know it! Even if we are really good spellers, it still happens from time to time that we misspell a word or hit the wrong keys. In the past, you had to run your texts (that you had written in Vim) through some sort of spell checker such as **Aspell** or **Ispell**. This was a tiresome process that could only be performed as a final task, unless you wanted to do it over and over again.

With version 7 of Vim, this troublesome way of spell checking is over. Now, Vim has got a built-in spell checker with support for more than 50 languages from around the world.

The new spell checker marks the wrongly written words as you type them in, so you know right away that there is an error.

The command to execute to turn on this helpful spell checker feature is:

```
:set spell
```

This turns on the spell checker with the default language (English). If you don't use English much and would prefer to use another language in the spell checker, then there is no problem changing this. Just add the code of the language you would like to use to the `spelllang` property. For example:

```
:set spelllang=de
```

Here, the language is set to German (Deutsch) as the spell checker language of choice. The language name can be written in several different formats. American English, for example, can be written as:

- en_us
- us
- American

Names can even be an industry-related name such as *medical*. If Vim does not recognize the language name, Vim will highlight it when you execute the property-setting command.

 If you change the `spelllang` setting to a language not already installed, then Vim will ask you if it should try to automatically retrieve it from the Vim homepage.

Personally, I tend to work in several different languages in Vim, and I really don't want to tell Vim all the time which language I am using right now.

Vim has a solution for this. By appending more language codes to the `spelllang` property (separated by commas), you can tell Vim to check the spelling in more than one language.

```
:set spelllang=en,da,de,it
```

Vim will then take the languages from the start to the end, and check if the words match any word in one of these languages. If they do, then they are not marked as a spelling error. Of course, this means that you can have a word spelled wrong in the language you are using but spelled correctly in another language, thereby introducing a hidden spelling error.

 You can find language packages for a lot of languages at the Vim FTP site: `ftp://ftp.vim.org/pub/vim/runtime/spell`.

Spelling errors are marked differently in Vim and Gvim.

In regular Vim, the misspelled word is marked with the `SpellBad` color group (normally, white on red).

In Gvim, the misspelled word is marked with a red curvy line underneath the word. This can, of course, be changed by changing the settings of the color group. (See the *Personal highlighting* section for more information.)

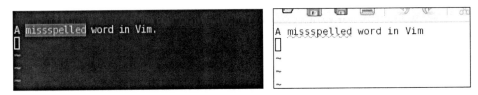

Whenever you encounter a misspelled word, you can ask Vim to suggest better ways to spell the word. This is simply done by placing the cursor over the word, going into the normal mode (press *Esc*), and then pressing *Z* + =.

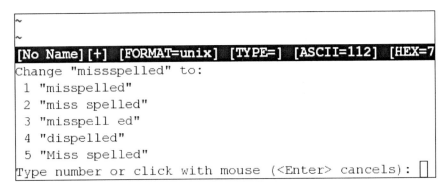

If possible, Vim will give you a list of good guesses for the word you were actually trying to write. In front of each suggestion is a number. Press the number you find in front of the right spelling (of the word you wanted) or press *Enter* if the word is not there.

Often Vim gives you a long list of alternatives for your misspelled word, but unless you have spelled the word completely wrong, chances are that the correct word is within the top five of the alternatives. If this is the case, and you don't want to look through the entire list of alternatives, then you can limit the output with the following command:

```
:set spellsuggest=X
```

Set x to the number of alternative ways of spelling you want Vim to suggest.

Adding helpful tool tips

In the *Modifying tabs* recipe, we learned about how to use tool tips to store more information using less space in the tabs in Gvim. To build on top of that same idea with this recipe, we move on and use tool tips in other places in the editor.

The editing area is the largest part of Vim. So, why not try to add some extra information to the contents of this area by using tool tips?

In Vim, tool tips for the editing area are called **balloons** and they are only shown when the cursor is hovering over one of the characters. The commands you will need to know in order to use the balloons are:

- The first command is the one you will use to actually turn on this functionality in Vim.

  `:set ballooneval`

- The second command tells Vim how long it should wait before showing the tool tip/balloon (the delay is in milliseconds and as a default is set to 600).

  `:set balloondelay=400`

- The last command is the one that actually sets the string that Vim will show in the balloon.

  `:set ballonexpr="textstring"`

  This can either be a static text string or the return of some function.

In order to have access to information about the place where you are hovering over a character in the editor, Vim provides access to a list of variables holding such information:

`v:beval_bufnr`	Number of the buffer in which the hovered area is
`v:beval_winnr`	Number of the window in which the hovered area is shown
`v:beval_lnum`	Line number on which the hovered character is situated
`v:beval_col`	Number of the column in which the hovered character is
`v:beval_text`	Word to which the hovered character is connected

So with these variables in hand, let's look at some examples.

Example 1:

The first example is based on one from the Vim help system. It shows how to make a simple function that will show the information from all the available variables.

```
function! SimpleBalloon()
    return 'Cursor is at line/column: ' . v:beval_lnum .
        \'/' . v:beval_col .
        \ ' in file ' .  bufname(v:beval_bufnr) .
        \ '. Word under cursor is: "' . v:beval_text . '"'
endfunction
set balloonexpr=SimpleBalloon()
set ballooneval
```

The result will look similar to the following screenshot:

```
362    endfunction
363    function! SimpleBalloon()
364        return 'Cursor is a|Cursor is at line/column: 363/21 in file .vimrc. Word under cursor is: "SimpleBalloon"|
365            \'/' . v:beval_col .
366        |\ ' in file ' .  bufname(v:beval_bufnr) .
367            \ '. Word under cursor is: "' . v:beval_text . '"'
```

Example 2:

Let's look at a more advanced example that explores the use of balloons for specific areas in editing. In this example, we will put together a function that gives us great information balloons for two areas at the same time:

- **Misspelled words**: The balloon gives ideas for alternative words
- **Folded text**: The balloon gives a preview of what's in the fold

So, let's take a look at what the function should look for, to detect if the cursor is hovering over either a misspelled word or a fold line (a single line representing multiple lines folded behind it).

In order to detect if a word is misspelled, the spell check would need to be turned on:

```
:set spell
```

If it is on, then calling the built-in spell checker function—spellsuggest()—would return alternative words if the hovered word was misspelled. So, to see if a word is misspelled, just check if the spellsuggest() returns anything. There is, however, a small catch. spellsuggest() also returns alternative, similar words if the word is not misspelled. To get around this, another function has to be used on the input word before putting it into the spellsuggest() function. This extra function is the spellbadword(). This basically moves the cursor to the first misspelled word in the sentence that it gets as input, and then returns the word. We just input a single word and if it is not misspelled, then the function cannot return any words. Putting no word into spellsuggest() results in getting nothing back, so we can now check if a word is misspelled or not.

It is even simpler to check if a word is in a line, in a fold. You simply have to call the foldclosed() function on the line number of the line over which the cursor is hovering (remember v:beval_lnum?), and it will return the number of the first line in the current fold; if not in a fold, then it returns -1. In other words, if foldclosed(v:beval_lnum) returns anything but -1 and 0, we are in a fold.

Putting all of this detection together and adding functionality to construct the balloon text ends up as the following function:

```
function! FoldSpellBalloon()
  let foldStart = foldclosed(v:beval_lnum )
  let foldEnd   = foldclosedend(v:beval_lnum)
  let lines = []
  " Detect if we are in a fold
  if foldStart < 0
    " Detect if we are on a misspelled word
    let lines = spellsuggest( spellbadword(v:beval_text)[ 0 ], 5, 0 )
  else
    " we are in a fold
    let numLines = foldEnd - foldStart + 1
    " if we have too many lines in fold, show only the first 14
    " and the last 14 lines
    if ( numLines > 31 )
      let lines = getline( foldStart, foldStart + 14 )
      let lines += [ '-- Snipped ' . ( numLines - 30 ) . ' lines --' ]
      let lines += getline( foldEnd - 14, foldEnd )
    else
      "less than 30 lines, lets show all of them
      let lines = getline( foldStart, foldEnd )
    endif
  endif
  " return result
```

```
    return join( lines, has( "balloon_multiline" ) ? "\n" : " " )
endfunction
set balloonexpr=FoldSpellBalloon()
set ballooneval
```

The result is some really helpful balloons in the editing area of Vim that can improve your work cycle tremendously. The following screenshot shows how the information balloon could look when it is used to preview a folded range of lines from a file:

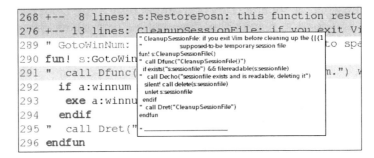

Instead, if the balloon is used on a misspelled word, it will look like the following screenshot:

In Chapter 4, *Production Boosters*, you can learn more about how to use folding of lines to boost productivity in Vim.

Using abbreviations

We all know the feeling of writing the same things over and over again, a dozen times during a day. This feeling is the exact opposite of what the philosophy of Vim tries to teach us.

The philosophy of Vim says that if you write a thing once, it is okay. However, if you're writing it twice or more times, then you should find a better way to do it.

One of the methods for getting around writing the same sentences over and over again is by using **abbreviations**.

In Vim, abbreviations are created with one of the following commands depending on which mode they should be available in:

- `:abbreviate`: Abbreviations for all modes
- `:iabbrev`: Abbreviations for the insert mode
- `:cabbrev`: Abbreviations for the command line only

All of the commands take two arguments—the abbreviation and the full text it should expand to.

So, let's start with a simple example of where the abbreviations can come in handy.

Example 1: Using abbreviations for quick address insertion

I have moved around a bit during the last few years, so a common task for me is writing messages where I tell about my new address. It didn't take me long before I had an abbreviation ready, so I didn't have to write the entire address.

Here is what it looked like:

```
:iabbrev myAddr 32 Lincoln Road, Birmingham B27 6PA, United Kingdom
```

Now every time I need to write my address, I just write `myAddr` and as soon as I press the *Space* key after the word, it expands to the entire address.

Vim is intelligent about detecting whether you are writing an abbreviation or it is just part of another word. This is why `myAddr` only expanded to the full address when I pressed the *Space* key after the word. If the character right after my abbreviation was a normal alphabetic letter, then Vim would know that I wasn't trying to use my abbreviation and it would not expand the word. The examples with the `abc` abbreviation are as follows.

`abc<space>` and `abc<enter>`	Both expand
`123abc<space>`	Will not expand as the abbreviation is part of a word
`abcd<space>`	Will not expand because there are letters after the abbreviation
`abc`	Will not expand until another special letter is pressed

A good place to keep your abbreviations so that you don't have to execute all the commands by hand is in a file in your VIMHOME. Simply place a file there—let's call it `abbreviations.vim` and write all your abbreviations in it. Then, in your `vimrc` file, just make sure that the file is read, which is done with the source command:

```
:source $VIM/abbreviations.vim
```

Every time you realize that you will need a new abbreviation, you first execute it and then you add it to your `abbreviations.vim`.

By now you have probably realized that you can use abbreviations for a lot of other interesting things. But anyway, here is a short list of examples to give you some ideas:

- Correct typical keypress errors:

  ```
  :iabbr teh the
  ```

- Simple templates for programming:

  ```
  :iabbr forx  for(x=0;x<100;x++){<cr><cr>}
  ```

- Easy commands in the command line:

  ```
  :cabbr csn colorscheme night
  ```

Getting used to adding your abbreviations to a file every time you find a new one might seem weird and inconvenient at first. At the end of the day, however, you will realize that it has saved you a lot of typing and that it will keep doing so. The only thing you have to do is add your abbreviations and reload the abbreviations file once in a while.

Sometimes, it can be annoying that abbreviations automatically change when you actually wanted to write something else. Let's say that you have an abbreviation for your address called "addr", but you actually want to write the word "addressed". In that case, your abbreviation would kick in and you would not be able to write the word easily.

A solution for this is to change your abbreviation to use a function that asks you whether or not to use the abbreviation before it actually inserts the word.

An example of such a function could be the following:

```
function! s:AbbrAsk(abbr,expansion)
  let answer = confirm("Use the abbreviation '" . a:abbr . "'?",
"&Yes\n&No", 1)
  return answer == 1 ? a:expansion : a:abbr
endfunction
```

The function is called `AbbrAsk` and takes two arguments. The first argument is the abbreviation and the second argument is the expanded abbreviation. For our address example, this function would be used as follows:

```
:iabbrev <expr> addr <SID>AbbrAsk('addr', "your full address
here")
```

So, now when you write the letters `addr`, you will be asked whether you would like to use the abbreviation or not.

Modifying key bindings

All of us have probably, at some point, used an editor other than Vim. Because of this, most of us have learned to use some very specific keyboard shortcuts for doing different tasks.

Even though the key bindings for the keyboard shortcuts in Vim are created with ease and use of speed in mind, sometimes it can still be faster to use the shortcuts you already know.

To facilitate this, Vim gives you the possibility to rebind almost every single key binding it has.

In this recipe, we will learn how to change the key bindings when using Vim in different modes.

The main commands to know when dealing with key bindings are:

- `:map`: For the **Normal, Insert, Visual,** and **Command-line** modes
- `:imap`: For the **Insert** mode only
- `:cmap`: For the **Command-line** mode only
- `:nmap`: For the **Normal** mode only
- `:vmap`: For the **Visual** mode only

Each of the command takes two arguments—the first is what keys the command should be bound to, and the second is the command to bind. So, let's look at an example.

Say you can't really get used to saving an open file by executing `:w` in the normal mode because you are used to using *Ctrl-S* to save a file and would like to keep it like that.

A mapping for this could be:

```
:map <C-s> :w<cr>
```

Notice the <C-s> in the key binding. This is the Vim way for writing 'key combination *Ctrl+S'*. Instead of *C (Ctrl)*, you could also use *A (Alt)* or *M (Meta)*. The <cr> at the end of the command is what actually executes the command. Without it, the command would simply be written to the command line but not executed.

There are several other special notations for some of the other keyboard keys. The following table shows the most common of them:

Keys	Notation
<BS>	Backspace
<Tab>	Tab
<CR>	Enter
<Enter>	Enter
<Return>	Enter
<Esc>	Escape
<Space>	Space
<Up>	Up arrow
<Down>	Down arrow
<Left>	Left arrow
<Right>	Right arrow
<F1> - <F12>	Function keys 1 to 12
#1, #2..#9,#0	Function keys F1 to F9, F10
<Insert>	Insert
<Del>	Delete
<Home>	Home
<End>	End
<PageUp>	Page up
<PageDown>	Page down

Maybe you only want to be able to save when you are in the insert mode and actually editing the file. To change the command for this, you only need to have the following:

```
:imap <C-s> <esc>:w<cr>a
```

So, what happens now is that you map the *Ctrl+S* to do a combination of key presses. First, press <esc> (the *Escape* key) to get out of the insert mode and into the normal mode. Then, use :w<cr> to execute the actual saving of the file, and finally the a to get back into the insert mode and go to the end of the line.

You could expand the mappings to fit all of the standard copy / paste / cut / save shortcuts from many applications. This could be constructed like this:

```
" save file (ctrl-s)
:map <C-s> :w<cr>
" copy selected text (ctrl-c)
:vmap <C-c> y
" Paste clipboard contents (ctrl-v)
:imap <C-p> <esc>P
" cut selected text (ctrl-x)
:vmap <C-x> x
```

If you are in Gvim, you can even get dialogs shown for the save-as and Open functionalities.

```
"Open new file dialog (ctrl-n)
    :map <C-n> :browse confirm e<cr>
"Open save-as dialog  (ctrl-shift-s)
    :map <C-S-s> :browse confirm saveas<cr>
```

You can get into a situation where you map a key combination in which the first key is actually bound to a function of its own. An example could be the $ key, which is bound to the "jump to end of line" functionality in Vim. You might, however, want to have a key binding like $1 for some functionality, $2 for some other functionality, and so on. The mapping could then look like:

```
:map   $1 :MyFunction1()<cr>
:map   $2 :MyFunction2()<cr>
```

Now when you press $, Vim will wait for one second after you press the $ key, and if it does not get the second character in the key binding before the timeout, it will execute the normal "jump to end of line" functionality. However, if you press *1* before the timeout, it will execute your Myfunction1() function instead.

With the ability to change the keyboard mapping in Vim, you really have an access to a powerful way of modifying the editor completely according to your needs.

 You can read more about mappings in the Vim help system under:
```
:help key-mapping.
```

Summary

In this chapter, we looked at how to make Vim a better editor for you by modifying it according to your personal needs.

We started by learning about how basic modifications of font and color scheme can give your editor a personalized look.

Then we dived a bit deeper into using colors for marking search matches, thereby making them easily recognizable.

To get the most out of an editor like Vim, you would often like it to have a large area for editing the files and less space spilled on the GUI. We looked at ways of modifying both the status line and tabs to be smaller and more informative.

Even though the menu bar and toolbar can be unimportant and just take up screen real estate, they can also be very useful additions to your editor. In this chapter, we learned how to add our own menu to the menu bar and even how to add icons that are full of functionality to the toolbar.

Many things can be done to the editing area to make it fit your personal needs. In this chapter, we looked at how to make it easier to get an overview of the editing area. Better and more visual cursors have been proposed, and line numbers have been added to the area.

We also looked at how to make the spell checker in Vim follow your preferred language, so that you will never again misspell a word. If using spell checker is not enough to correct your errors, then maybe the use of abbreviations can help you.

Finally, we looked at how we can change the key bindings in Vim in such a way that it will react on keyboard shortcuts you are used to from other editors.

You have a fully personalized Vim editor with all the recipes in this chapter and you are now ready to move on and learn more about how you can optimize your navigation around the files in Vim.

3

Better Navigation

Working with large files, or many files at the same time, can be a troublesome task. Sometimes, you realize that you waste more time looking for content to edit than doing the actual editing.

The philosophy of Vim is all about not wasting our valuable time, so Vim has means for optimizing the way we navigate files.

In this chapter, we will look at some of the ways in which Vim helps us easily navigate through our files, whether we're dealing with one file or fifty files. Some recipes use marks to mark a spot for later return, while others use search techniques to find the place you are looking for.

The recipes in this chapter cover the following areas:

- Faster navigation in a file
- Faster navigation in the Vim help system
- Faster navigation in multiple buffers
- Faster lookup of files using the Vim file explorer
- In-file searching
- Searching in multiple files or buffers with `vimgrep`
- Using marks as a tool for navigation
- Using signs as a tool to get a better overview

After reading this chapter, you should be able to boost your navigation speed and have no problems finding the files you are looking for.

Faster navigation in a file

Sometimes even the simplest of tasks, like navigating through a single file, can be optimized. Vim offers several methods of navigation within a file, which can adapt to the contents of the file and how it is organized. Some of these methods are obvious, while others are more complex.

Context-aware navigation

Mostly, the files we are editing are well structured. If our files are text, then this structure can be in the form of paragraphs, sentences, and words, or at other times code with functions, blocks, and code lines.

Vim supports jumping around the file according to the structure in the file. It also has key bindings that make it easy to go to the exact place in the file.

Let's look at some examples:

- Moving around within a text file
- Moving in a code file

Moving around within a code file

You are working on a normal text file and in the middle of a sentence you realize that you have forgotten to make the first letter in the paragraphs uppercase. You could, of course, use the arrow keys or the $H \mid J \mid K \mid L$ navigation keys to move to the beginning of the paragraph to correct this. However, it would be faster to just press the following in the normal mode:

{

You are now placed at the beginning of the paragraph, or in the empty line just above it (if one exists). Now, you go into the normal mode by pressing the *Esc* key and then use the { movement command to go to the beginning of the paragraph. The same can be applied if you want to go back to the end of the paragraph—you simply have to use the counterpart of {, namely:

}

Maybe you were not actually working at the end of the paragraph, but rather on correcting some text in the middle of the paragraph. Vim remembers where you were making changes to the file previously (and actually up to 999 of the last places you have changed something) and you can ask it to take you back to the correct place. Just use the following command in the normal mode:

g,

Using this command several times in a row will loop you through locations of previous changes in the file. As with the { command, this command also has a counterpart that moves forward through the list of recent locations where changes have taken place. The command for this is:

`g;`

Vim will alert you if you get to one of the ends of the list of changes.

Maybe it wasn't at the beginning of the paragraph that you forgot to capitalize a letter, but rather at the beginning of the current sentence. Again, Vim helps you move faster and offers you a pair of commands to move to the beginning and end of the current sentence. The commands are as follows:

- (: Move to the beginning of the sentence
-): Move to the end of the sentence

Vim doesn't want us to waste any time when working with it. Even though you could easily go through the letters of a word by simply using the arrow keys, Vim still thinks this is waste of key presses and instead offers a set of commands for word movement such as:

- *w*: Move to the beginning of the next word
- *b*: Move to the beginning of the previous word
- *e*: Move to the end of the word

These commands can be combined such that if you want to go to the end of the next word, you simply press:

`we`

When it comes to what a word actually consists of, Vim has two definitions. In Vim we have:

- A word consisting of alphabetic letters, numbers, dashes, and underscores
- A WORD consisting of any character except whitespaces (tab and space)

The previously mentioned movement commands work on word, and of course Vim has the same commands available for WORD. Simply use the same commands, but use them in uppercase instead (for example, use w to go to the beginning of the next word).

If you want to execute one of the commands mentioned in this section more than once in a row, simply add the number of times you want it executed in front of the command. For example, 5g to go to the place you changed something five changes ago.

Moving in a code file

Compared to text files, code does not have any paragraphs or sentences to navigate through. It does, however, frequently contain a lot of structures and blocks, each of which has a very specific contextual meaning within the code. An example could be the simple code block:

```
If( a == b)
  {
    print "a and b are the same";
  }
```

Here, the line with print is within the context of the if block surrounding it.

Because Vim is the favorite editor of many programmers, it offers a lot of movement commands to use when you are working with code. Common for all of them is that the parts of the code you want to jump between need to have a contextual connection to each other.

A simple example could be a construction such as the #if-#else-#endif construction from the C programming language. Here we have a beginning (#if), an end (#endif) and a midpoint (#else).

So, if you are in the line with #if and press the following command:

%

You will go to the #else part. Pressing it again will take you to the #endif, and yet another execution of the command will get you back to the #if.

Vim does not know all programming language constructs, but by default it knows most of the contextual constructs of the C programming language. Besides this, it knows the normal block construction methods from most programming languages — the use of parentheses and brackets (for example, { is the block start and } is the block end).

If you want Vim to know the constructs of many other programming languages, then install the mtchit plugin. This plugin is available with Vim as of version 7.0, but can also be found at http://www.vim.org/ scripts/.

Simply by knowing the programmer's common use of parentheses / brackets, Vim can provide us with several useful navigation commands. This means that as long as the code uses some start parenthesis / bracket to begin a block and the counterpart to end it, Vim will understand it.

Let's say you are in a function that consists of many lines and you want to go to the beginning of the function. Mostly, the brackets surrounding the contents of a function are the outermost pair of brackets around the place in the file where you currently are (given that you are editing the current function). So, for Vim to find the beginning of the function, it simply has to find the outermost bracket pair and then go to the opening bracket.

```
function myExample() {
    ...many lines of code...
      /* cursor is placed at the beginning of this line */
    ...many lines of code...
}
```

In the previous example, the % command would take us to the closing bracket and pressing it again would take us to the opening bracket. But, what if the cursor was actually placed inside another pair of brackets? In that case, the % command would only move the cursor to them, and not the beginning of the function.

Again, Vim has some handy commands for you:

- [[and][: Move backwards / forward to the next section beginning (for example, start of a function)
- [] and]]: Move backwards / forward to the next section end (for example, end of a function)

Executing these commands multiple times in a row takes you to the beginning / end of the next / previous section, and therefore gives you a convenient way of cycling through the functions in a file.

So if you have two or more functions in the file and the cursor is currently at the beginning of the first function, pressing [key twice will take you to the beginning of the next function, and so on. If you want to go back to the previous function, you just have to press]] and Vim will take you right back to the beginning of the previous function.

Note that in most object-oriented languages, the class beginning / end is often the outermost section.

Often, you just want to go to the beginning of the current block (for example, the beginning of a `while` loop) because it is here that you have defined all the local variables for the scope of this block. For this also, Vim has a set of movement commands:

- [{: Move to the beginning of the block
-]}: Move to the end of the block

If the block in the code is a comment, then it does not have any brackets around it. So Vim cannot use the brackets to navigate to its beginning /end.

Therefore, Vim has some special movement commands for comment blocks:

- [/: Move to the beginning of the comment block
-]/: Move to the end of the comment block

By default, not all comment formats are supported by Vim. It supports the comment formats used in the C programming language (/* */), C++ (//), and in many scripting languages (#). However, it is possible to add support for extra comment formats when you add support for the syntax of new programming languages.

Sometimes, when you work on a piece of code, you tend to forget how a variable is actually defined. Vim has a command that can help you look up the definition of the variable (or the first occurrence of it, in the case of interpreted languages such as Python) if it is defined in the current file. The command is as follows, and should be entered while the cursor is placed on the variable name you want to look up:

`gd`

This command is easy to remember if you just think of the phrase "Goto Declaration" and take the first letter from the two words.

What this command actually does is that it starts by going to the beginning of the current section (remember the [[command) because this is where the local definitions are normally placed. Then, it makes a search forward in the file for the first occurrence of the variable name. If it does not find it before reaching the place where you started the lookup, then it moves to the first line of the file and again searches forward in the file looking for any global definitions of the variable. If it still does not find the definition, then Vim does a * search for the variable in the file (read more about the * search in the *Search and you will find* section).

If you know that the variable is globally defined, or if you want the global definition of the variable, then Vim has a command that starts by looking from line one of the file, instead of looking in the current section first. The command is:

gD

Vim is naturally smart enough to ignore any references to the variable in comment blocks because these are definitely not the declaration of the variable.

If Vim finds the variable definition (or the first available usage of the variable in the file), then it moves the cursor to this place.

 Put 1 in front of the gd command (like 1gd) if you want Vim to ignore all the matches that are inside a { } block that ends before the current cursor position (for example, in another function block earlier in the file).

Navigating long lines

Some like their long lines visually wrapped in Vim, while others want them to extend beyond the border of the editor (that is, not shown). Personally, I like to have my text lines wrapped because it makes the overview of the text a lot better. However, this does introduce an irritating problem. If you have a long line and it is wrapped, then the wrapped part shows up as a new line in the visualization of the file contents. This is not a problem in itself, but navigating to the wrapped part of the line is. If you use the arrow keys, or J / K to navigate between the lines, then it simply ignores the wrapped part of the line and goes directly to the next actual line in the file. If you dislike this behavior, then here's a short little recipe to fix this problem.

I have discovered that if I hold down the *Alt* key while I use the up / down arrows to navigate the lines in the file, then Vim should follow the lines as shown visually in Vim, and not as the actual lines in the file. The key mappings to make this work are as follows and should simply be added to your vimrc file:

```
map <A-DOWN> gj
map <A-UP> gk
imap <A-UP> <ESC>gki
imap <A-DOWN> <ESC>gji
```

The mapping works in the normal mode and the insert mode. If you want this to happen without having to remember to hold down the *Alt* key, then simply remove the A- part of the key combination to which the commands are mapped (for example, map <DOWN> gj).

Faster navigation in Vim help

Vim comes with a very useful and comprehensive help system that you have probably by now already played around with. What you might not know, however, is that the help system comes with a hyperlink support that resembles the hyperlinks we know from the Internet. There are two types of links—subject links marked as "some subject" and option links marked as "option".

A subject link refers to the beginning of a section in the help system, whereas the option links take you directly to the description of a certain option. When you place the cursor on a link, you can press *Ctrl+]* to follow the link no matter what type of link it is. This is very nice, but if you are using a non-English keyboard layout, the key for *]* is often not available with a single key press. In this case, it could be nice to remap the key to some other key. In an Internet browser, you could navigate to a link and press *Enter*, and to reflect this you could have a mapping like the following:

```
nmap <buffer> <CR> <C-]>
```

If you are in a browser and want to return to the previous page you visited, then you can press the Backspace key. It would be nice to have this in the Vim help system. Hence, a mapping like the following could be useful:

```
nmap <buffer> <BS> <C-T>
```

Now we can move forward and backward in the hyperlinks in the help system with easy-to-remember key bindings. Now, let's also add some easy navigation keys for finding the next / previous place where a subject or an option link is situated in the currently open `help` file. This way we can easily scroll through the `help` file until we find what we are looking for.

```
nmap <buffer> o /''[a-z]\{2,\}''<CR>
nmap <buffer> O ?''[a-z]\{2,\}''<CR>
nmap <buffer> s /\|\S\+\|<CR>
nmap <buffer> S ?\|\S\+\|<CR>
```

Now you can press *o* to go to next place where an option link is, or *s* if you want to go to the next subject link. The same is available if you want to move backwards. You just have to press the capital letters instead—hence, *O* for the previous option link and *S* for the previous subject link.

 To prevent the mappings from interfering with other key mappings, you can add them to a file called `help.vim` and place it in `$VIMHOME/ftplugin/`.

So now, we are only missing a final bit of our improved help system navigation. We need a way to open the help system a bit faster. Normally, when you press the *F1* key, the help system opens on the default page. However, it would be nice if the key did a lookup of the word currently under the cursor. So let's look at a key mapping for this:

```
:map <F1> <ESC>:exec "help ".expand("<cWORD>")<CR>
```

This one is a bit hard. As the `:help` command is normally used for looking up Vim commands, the commands on the line after the `:help` are not interpreted. Because of this, we have to wrap the command in the `:exec` command.

To get the word under the cursor, we use `<cWORD>`. The `WORD` part is in uppercase, which means that all characters except whitespaces (space and tab) can be part of the word. This is needed because Vim commands can contain special characters other than alphanumeric (think of, if you were to look up `<cWORD>`).

This key mapping can be used from outside the help system and could, therefore, be added to your `vimrc` file, and not placed in `help.vim`.

Faster navigation in multiple buffers

Often, you are not just working on one file, but have multiple files open. For every file you have open, you have a Vim buffer. A buffer can be shown or hidden, which means that to find the file you want to work on, you will need to find the buffer containing it.

You could, of course, bring up the list of buffers and find the right buffer in the list. To show the list of buffers, you can use the command:

```
:buffers
```

This list is not interactive. So in order to select the buffer you want to go to, you need to look up the number at the beginning of the line where the file is listed. This is the number of the buffer where the file is placed. With this number, you can now go directly to the buffer by executing the following command:

```
:buffer N
```

where N is the number of the buffer.

This way of navigating the buffers is not always the most efficient. You could also cycle through the buffers using the following commands:

- `:bnext`
- `:bprevious`

Even though these commands can be accessed through their shorter names :bn and :bp, they are still commands you have to write in the normal mode. This means that it takes at least five key presses to execute the command, which is not convenient.

So, in order to make this buffer cycling a lot faster, you could add the following mapping to your vimrc file:

```
map <C-right> <ESC>:bn<CR>
map <C-left> <ESC>:bp<CR>
```

What these map lines do is make it possible to use *Ctrl*+left arrow key to go to previous buffer and *Ctrl*+right arrow key to go to next buffer. So, by holding down *Ctrl* while pressing the left / right keys repetitively, you can easily and quickly cycle through the files you have open.

 If you want to toggle back and forth between the current and previous buffer, you can use *Ctrl+6* (*Ctrl+o Ctrl+6* if in the insert mode) or :e #.

Open referenced files faster

In many programming languages, you can include other files in the current file, and thereby split the contents across multiple files. Often, the inclusion of the file resembles something like:

```
#include "somefile.h"
```

Here, we have "somefile.h" as the name of the file we included.

It would be nice to have an easy way to open the included file. Vim has a command that helps you in doing exactly that. Move the cursor to the place in the file where the filename of the file you want to open is, and execute the following command in the normal mode:

gf

You can remember this command by thinking of the goto file. Vim looks for the file in several different places as follows:

- Vim looks in the places it has defined in the path option and relative to the currently open file
- If not found, Vim uses the suffixadd function to see if it can find the file by adding one of the suffixes (for example, adding .c to the filename)

- If still not found, Vim uses the `includeexpr` expression to convert the filename to something that is hopefully understandable as a filename (for example, `java.com.http` is translated to `java/com/http.java`).

If Vim finds the file, it opens the file in the current buffer; and if not, it returns an error message. If the buffer you are currently in is not saved, or if anything else is going on such that Vim cannot abandon the currently open file, then Vim cannot open the file. This can be quite annoying, but it is a problem we can prevent from happening. By simply adding the following command to your `vimrc` file, you will always open the new file in another buffer and Vim does not have to abandon the currently open file:

```
:map gf :edit <cfile><CR>
```

This command simply overwrites the `gf` command and instead opens the file under the cursor with the `:edit` command. If it does not exist, this command opens a new empty buffer.

 If you want Vim to support filenames with spaces when using `gf`, add the following to your `vimrc`: `set isfname+=32`.

`32` is the decimal number representing space in the ASCII table.

Search and you will find

We all know the feeling of having seen the things we have misplaced somewhere, but not remembering exactly where. What we normally do in a situation like this is search for the thing we are missing.

In Vim, we can do the exact same thing. Let's split the search into three cases as follows:

- Searches in the current file
- Searches in multiple files
- Searches in the help files

In the following sections, we will look at recipes that help you with the three types of search.

Search the current file

Even though your file might not be that long, it can still be a pain to find something you are looking for. Vim has several ways to help you find what you are looking for.

So, let's look at some examples.

Example 1: Find the next occurrence of a word

You know that you have the text you are looking for somewhere near the word "someWord". To find this, you simply need to perform a search for it by executing the following command in the normal mode:

`?someWord`

The command searches backwards in the file for the first occurrence of the word after the question mark. If you are at the end of the file, this is the perfect way to search for a word. However, if you are at the beginning of the file it would make more sense to search forward in the file. This is done by exchanging the question mark for a slash:

`/someWord`

The word might be in the file several times, and maybe the first place you found wasn't the place you were looking for. No worries. You simply need to press *n* to go to the next occurrence of the word in the direction of the search. If you would rather change the direction, simply press *N* instead and it will find the preceding occurrence of the word.

If you want to do the same search again, simply use `??` or `//` instead of writing the entire word again.

If you add set `incsearch`, your search will be live and the cursor will start jumping through the file as you type. Every time you input the next character of the search word, the cursor location will be moved to the next / previous occurrence of a word matching the search word.

 You have to press *Enter* in order to actually execute the search in the end, or else the cursor will go back to where it came from. To cancel a search and go back to where you came from, you can simply press the *Esc* key.

Example 2: Search for a word under the cursor

If you are already near one occurrence of the word you are looking for, but it is just not the right one, or maybe you want to look through all places where a certain word is used and the word is already written, why use extra key presses on writing the word again? Vim has just the right commands for you. Place the cursor on or just in front of the word you want to search for, and press either of the following two keys in the normal mode:

#

*

The first one searches for the previous occurrence of the word under the cursor, and the second one searches for the next occurrence of the word. Pressing the key multiple times jumps to the next / previous occurrence of the word repeatedly. This makes it really fast to jump through all occurrences of the word.

Maybe your word isn't actually a complete word, but just a part of a word. Vim has a command for this too. Simply press the following key combination in the normal mode:

g#

g*

Now Vim not just jumps to the next occurrence of the word, but also to any occurrences where the word is part of another word. For example, placing the cursor on the word "foo" and pressing g# will make Vim jump to the next "foo" in both "foobar" and "food".

Search in multiple files

Maybe what you are looking for is not in the current file. Maybe you are not even sure which file you should be looking in to find what you are looking for. On a Unix-flavored operating system like GNU / Linux, you typically have the command-line tool grep that looks for certain words or patterns in all the files specified. In Microsoft Windows, there is a similar tool available as the FIND and FINDSTR commands. However, these are not commonly used by Windows users. In order to provide all Vim users (no matter which platform) with a way to search through files, Vim has its very own grep command. The command to use is:

```
:vimgrep /pattern/[j][g] file file2... fileN
```

This command takes two arguments. The first is the pattern you want to search for. You can use Vim's regular expressions in the pattern or you can just write a word. The pattern needs to be enclosed in /, and after the last / you can add either of the two flags j and g. The flags help you select how much to get in your result, and how it should be presented to you.

Instead of / around your pattern, you can use any non-ID character. A non-ID character is any character not defined in the isindent option.

If the g flag is added, then the result will include a line for each match of the pattern. This means that if your pattern is matched three times in the same line, then you will get the line three times in your result. If the j flag is added to the end of your pattern, then you will not be presented with the result. It will just be updated into your **quickfix** list for later retrieval (see :help quickfix for more information about quickfix lists). Without the j flag, you will be moved directly to the first match and the rest of the result will be added to your quickfix list.

To show your quickfix list with the vimgrep result, simply use the :clist command or navigate to next / previous match with :cnext / :cprevious.

The second argument to the vimgrep command is the list of files you want to search through. The file list can consist of a single filename, a list of filenames, or a pattern using the star wildcard (for example, *.c *.h). You can also use the ** wildcard such as **/*.c if you want to search in all the C files in the current folder, and recursively through all subdirectories.

```
:clist..
 1 Desktop/diverse/fpix-0.90.1/driver/finepix-main.c:309 col 95: dev_err
            rame. Please, report to driver maintainer.\n");
 2 Desktop/diverse/fpix-0.90.1/userspace/fpix-stress-v412.c:3 col 13: *
 3 Desktop/diverse/fpix-0.90.1/userspace/fpix-stress-v412.c:19 col 5: in
 4 Desktop/diverse/fpix-0.90.1/userspace/fpix.c:3 col 13: * Public domai
 5 Desktop/diverse/fpix-0.90.1/userspace/fpix.c:44 col 5: int main(void)
 6 Desktop/diverse/fpix-0.90.1/userspace/fpixtest.c:3 col 13: * Public d
 7 Desktop/diverse/fpix-0.90.1/userspace/fpixtest.c:16 col 5: int main(v
 8 Desktop/diverse/fuji-finepixa310-test/stream.c:255 col 5: int main(in
 9 bin/bin2iso.c:29 col 5: int main( int argc, char **argv )
10 bluemote/bluemote.c:56 col 5: int main(int argc, char *argv[])
11 bluemote/bluemote.c:147 col 11: if(init_mainmenu()==-1) continue;
12 bluemote/bluemote.c:261 col 10: int init_mainmenu()
13 bluemote/bluemote.c:291 col 22: while((ret = init_mainmenu())==0);
14 bluemote/mouse.c:75 col 1: main (int argc, char **argv)
15 btsco/a2play.c:536 col 5: int main(int argc, char *argv[])
:vimgrep /main/ **/*.c
```

Search the help system

Sometimes when you need help for something in Vim, you might not know what exactly you should look for. Of course, you could start going through the entire help system, but it consists of several different files and thousands of possible keywords.

So, Vim has the right command to help you out here. As in the previous recipe, the keyword is grep, and for the Vim help system it is centered around the following command:

```
:helpgrep pattern [@LANG]
```

The command takes one argument, the pattern you search for, plus one optional argument to limit the language. Let's look at an example to make it clearer. You need some information on autocompletion, but you do not know where to look for it. As English is the only language you understand, you would want the help to be in the same language. A search for this could look like the following:

```
:helpgrep completion@en
```

What the command does is search for the word completion through all the English (en) documentation. The command takes you to the first match it finds, and the rest of the matches are added to the quickfix list for later retrieval.

 If you want to use the location list instead of the quickfix list for your result, then you can use the :lhelpgrep command instead.

The helpgrep command does not actually look through all the documentation when searching, but uses a tag list containing tags for all the available documentation to look up a pattern. This tag list is, however, not created automatically. So it is important to note that if you install a Vim plugin that has its own documentation, then you need to use the following command:

```
:helptags /path/to/documentation
```

The path to the documentation only needs to be where you have installed the new documentation. But in order for the Vim to actually be able to find the documentation, it has to be in a docs/ directory in one of the places defined in the runtimepath in Vim (see :help 'runtimepath').

X marks the spot

Sometimes when editing a line in a file, you have to go somewhere else in the file to look up something. Afterwards, it can be difficult to find the line you were editing, and you waste valuable time.

Wouldn't it be nice if you could mark the spot before leaving it, such that it is easy to find later?

Vim has some tools for you that can do just that. We can split it into two categories:

* Visible markers
* Hidden markers

In the following two sections, we will look at the possible ways of adding marks in Vim, and then it's up to you to figure out which one fits your needs the best.

Visible markers—using signs

In Vim, we have a nice feature for marking a line with a visible mark—signs. A sign is a mark that will show up in the leftmost column in the editor.

 If you want to change the color of the column in which the sign is shown, then you can use the following command:

`:highlight SignColumn guibg=darkgrey`

Depending on whether you are using Vim in a console or as Gvim, the sign can be either a combination of characters (for example, >>) or an icon. To use the signs, you will need a bit of setting up. You only have to do this once if you have it in your `vimrc` file.

The first thing you have to do is define the signs you want to have. The command you need to use is as follows:

`:sign define name arguments`

The arguments can be one of the following:

* `linehl`: The color group you want to mark the line with.
* `text`: The text used as a sign in console Vim (for example, >> !! or ++). A maximum of two characters can be used per sign.
* `texthl`: The color group you want the sign text marked with.

- icon: The full path to the icon you want for the sign in Gvim. The icon should be small enough to fit the size of only two characters. The format should be a bitmap format, but `.xpm` format is preferred.

An example could be:

```
:sign define information text=!> linehl=Warning texthl=Error icon=/path/
to/information.xpm
```

Now, we have defined a sign and have added it to our `vimrc` file, and we are ready to place the sign somewhere. The command is:

```
:exe ":sign place 123 line=" . line(.) ."name=information file=" .
expand("%:p")
```

Replace the number `123` with any number you will use as ID for this sign.

As you can see, this is a bit harder; but it can easily be mapped to a key.

What it does is add the sign named `information` under the ID 123 to the current line (`line(.)`) in the currently open file (`expand("%:p")`). Mapping this to a line is as follows:

```
:map <F7> :exe ":sign place 123 line=" . line(".") ."name=information
file=" . expand("%:p")<CR>
```

This maps the information sign to the *F7* key such that it will be placed in the current line whenever you press the *F7* key.

Sometimes, we also want to remove the sign again. In Vim, this is called to "unplace" a sign:

```
:sign unplace ID
```

The ID is the ID you gave your sign when you placed it (123 in the previous example). This removes the sign from all the places where you have added the sign with that ID. You might want to remove it only from the current file, and can therefore add another argument for the file like this:

```
:sign unplace ID file=name
```

Or you can use this to remove the sign from the buffer:

```
:sign unplace ID buffer=bufferno.
```

Here, `bufferno` is the number of the current buffer (see `:buffers`).

If you want to remove the sign in the current line, then you can simply use:

```
:sign unplace
```

Let's map this to *Ctrl-F7* just to make it symmetric with the sign placement mapping we have defined earlier:

```
:map <C-F7> :sign unplace<CR>
```

 If you have added several signs with the same ID to a file, then the previous mapping will only remove the uppermost sign with the specific ID and not the one in the current line.

As this is a chapter about navigation, we also need to know a bit about navigating to a sign. This is called **sign-jumping** in Vim and uses the following command:

```
:sign jump ID file=file
```

Here ID is the ID of the sign you want to jump to and `file` is the file you want to find the sign in. Instead of `file=file`, you can use `buffer=bufferno`.

Again, if the sign has been added with the same ID several times in the file / buffer, then it will jump to the first sign in the file.

 Paul Rouget has created a Vim script that makes the usage of signs a lot easier. You can find it here: `http://www.vim.org/scripts/script.php?script_id=1580`.

Hidden markers—using marks

Marks is a fast and easy way to add a mark to the current line so that you can later jump to it easily. Basically, it consists of a normal mode command that sets the mark and a normal mode command to jump to the mark. You won't be able to see if a line is marked or not unless you open the list of marks.

So, let's look at how to mark the current line. We simply press the *m* key in the normal mode followed by one of these characters—*0-9*, *a-z*, or *A-Z*. For instance, if you press *m* + *a* it means that the current line is marked with the mark named "a". If you later want to jump to this line, then you simply press '+*a* (single quote + mark name) and you will be taken to the beginning of the line you marked (if indented, then to just before the first non-whitespace character).

In some cases it might not be efficient to be placed at the beginning of the line, but it would be much better to be placed where you were when you added the mark. To jump to this place instead, you simply replace the single quote with a ` (backtick) like `+*a*.

The different mark names have different meanings and work areas as follows:

Mark	Usage
0-9	These are marks set from .viminfo and normally only used by Vim itself (for example, mark 0 is the place where cursor was when the file was last exited). A user can, however, use this to make an "open recently used" functionality.
a-z	These are marks only available in the current file. These marks are deleted when the file is closed. You can only jump to a lowercase mark if you are inside the buffer containing the file.
A-Z	These are marks available across files. These marks can be jumped to even if you are not in the file where the mark is situated. If a viminfo file is available, then these marks are saved until next time you edit a file.

You can always get a complete list of your marks by using the following command:

`:marks`

This shows which files the different marks are set in and on what lines. To delete one or more marks, you can use the command:

`:delmarks markid markid...markid`

The examples of how it can be used are:

`:delmarks a b c`

`:delmarks a-c`

```
:delmarks a f-i 1-4
```

If you want to delete all marks in the current buffer, then simply use the command:

```
:delmarks!
```

Other types of marks are set by Vim all the time when using it. These can be marks for where the cursor was the last time the insert mode was exited, beginning / end of text selected in the visual mode, the last place you changed something, and so on.

Look in `:help mark-motions` for more information on how to use marks and which other types of marks you have available.

Summary

In this chapter, we looked at alternative ways for boosting the speed at which we navigate through files and buffers in Vim.

First, we looked at how to navigate through a single file faster by using the contextual structure of the file for navigation. We also looked at a nice recipe for how we can make it easier to navigate files with long, wrapped lines.

Next, we looked at how to to navigate the Vim help system faster and learned how simple key bindings can make the help navigation more intuitive and recognizable.

Now we knew how to navigate inside a file, but we also needed to know how to navigate between files and buffers. The next section took us through how to navigate the buffers faster and how to open a file that is referenced by another file with only two key presses.

We can navigate in many ways, and in the preceding sections we looked at how to use the search mechanisms in Vim to navigate not only the open files, but also files on the disk. We also learned how to use searches in the help system to find help on topics we could not find normally.

Finally, we have looked at how to use signs and marks to jump around in files, and how Vim helps us simply by adding some marks automatically when we use it.

So, we have learned how to navigate around in a file faster with Vim. You are now ready to move to the next chapter where we will take a look at how to boost your productivity by using even more of the built-in Vim functionality.

4
Production Boosters

In this chapter, we will look at how even small changes can make work go faster and more smoothly in Vim. Some recipes introduce you to features in Vim, while others will show you how scripts can help.

It doesn't matter whether you use Vim for making small changes to configuration files, or if you use it as your primary editor in a large development project. You will find recipes in this chapter that can help you improve your performance when using Vim.

This chapter contains recipes that cover the following topics:

- Templates using simple template files
- Templates using abbreviations
- Autocompletion using known words and tag lists
- Autocompletion using omnicompletion
- Vim macros and macro recording
- Using sessions
- Project management using sessions
- Registers and undo branches
- Folding for better overview and outlining
- vimdiff for change tracking
- Opening files everywhere using netrw

After reading this chapter, you should be able to boost your productivity in Vim by several percent.

Using templates

No matter what type of files you are working with, there are always some basic things to set up when starting off with a new file. Creating this setup is a tedious task, and even worse is the fact that you have to do it again when you start on a new file. So, why spend a lot of time on these things when you could just as well create templates for these types of structural patterns?

In the next couple of sections, we will look at recipes for different types of templates. Some templates will be file-type specific while others will be using user input to trigger small-content templates (for example, code snippets used by programmers).

So, let's get started on creating some templates.

Using template files

Every time you start working on a new file, it is most likely that the first thing you'll do is add some sort of header (or other information) to the file. What you have to add is, of course, dependent on which file type you are working on. Some examples could be as follows:

- Adding basic structure (`<html>`, `<head>`, and `<body>`) to new HTML files
- Adding a header to all C files and also a main function to the `main.c` files
- Adding the main class structure to a Java file

You can probably find many other things you would like to add to the file types you work with.

So, how do we create a template file? Let's use an HTML file template as an example. The structure in such a file is quite static, and hence great to have a template for. Our simple template could look like:

```
<html>
    <head>
        <title></title>
        <meta name="generator" content="Vim" />
        <meta name="author" content="Kim Schulz"/>
    </head>
    <body>
        <p>Content goes here...</p>
    </body>
</html>
```

We create a directory in our VIMHOME called `templates/` and place a file with the previous HTML code in the directory. We save the file as `html.tpl`.

Now the first template is in place, but we need to get it loaded into all-new HTML files that we create. To do so, we add the following auto-command to our `vimrc` file:

```
:autocmd BufNewFile *.html 0r $VIMHOME/templates/html.tpl
```

This command ensures that when you create a new file with the `*.html` file extension, the content of your template file is read into your new file. This way your file gets prepared with the template's content before you can start editing it.

All this is very nice, but after adding a bunch of templates, you might get tired of adding lines to your `vimrc` file. So, let's make our first line a bit more intelligent:

```
:autocmd BufNewFile * silent! 0r $VIMHOME/templates/%:e.tpl
```

What this single line does is that whenever you open a file, it looks for a template that matches the extension of the file. For example, when creating the `index.html` file, it looks in `$VIMHOME/templates/` for a file named `html.tpl`.

If there is no template for the file type, then it simply creates an empty file as usual.

Let's take these templates even further by adding support for placeholders (for places where you want to add text to the file, fast). A placeholder could look very different depending on what you like, but I propose something like `<+KEYWORD+>`. So, if we take a line from the HTML template mentioned previously and add a placeholder to it, it would look like this:

```
<html>
  <head>
     <title><+TITLE+></title>
     <meta name="generator" content="<+GENERATOR+>" />
     <meta name="author" content="<+AUTHOR+>"/>
  </head>
  <body>
     <p><+CONTENT+></p>
  </body>
</html>
```

Now, we have the placeholders in place and only need a way to jump between them. So, let's add a command to our `vimrc` that will make it easy to make this jump. We want to use *Ctrl+j* as the jump key binding because it can easily be used in the insert mode and *j* (for jump) makes it easy to remember. The command could look like this:

```
nnoremap <c-j> /<+.\{-1,}+><cr>c/+>/e<cr>
inoremap <c-j> <ESC>/<+.\{-1,}+><cr>c/+>/e<cr>
```

Now, you can easily jump to the next placeholder in the file, change the text, and jump on to the next placeholder simply by pressing the *Ctrl-j* text, the *Ctrl-j* text, and so on.

By having the keyword in the placeholder, you can easily see what you are supposed to add there.

 You can mark your placeholders by adding a match command to your vimrc: `match Todo /<+.\++>/` (replace `Todo` with whatever color group you like).

Abbreviations as templates

In the previous section, we learned how to make templates for entire file types. So now, let's look at how to make templates for patterns inside the file content itself.

In Chapter 2, *Personalizing Vim*, we briefly looked at how to use abbreviations for limiting the amount of key presses whenever possible. Now, let's take the idea of using abbreviations and copy it to our template system. Let's look at the command and what it's all about, just to refresh our memory:

```
:iabbrev match replace-string
```

We only want this command to work in insert mode as this is where the pattern templates should be used. An example could be the following pattern template for a C file:

```
:iabbrev <buffer> for( for (x=0;x<var;x++){<cr><cr>}
```

This gives us a nice little `for` loop whenever we input `for(` in the contents of the file. The `(` is added to prevent manually written `for` loops from being converted. The inserted content will look like this:

```
for (x=0;x<var;x++)
   {
   }
```

 Having `<buffer>` in front of an abbreviation limits its availability to the current buffer.

As you can see, this is quite static code. In order to make it a bit more flexible, let's use the placeholder concept we introduced in the previous section.

Because the placeholders in this case are more like jump points, we simplify them to be just <+++>. Besides this, we need one single placeholder for where the cursor should be placed after inserting the pattern template. In case of the previous example, it would be nice to have the cursor placed right after the start parenthesis.

So to make this work, we introduce the `!cursor!` placeholder and the command will look like this:

```
iabbrev for( for(!cursor!;<+++>;<+++>){<cr><+++><cr>}<Esc>
:call search('!cursor!','b')<cr>cf!:
```

(All of the previous command should be on one line.)

Now, whenever the `for(` abbreviation is written, the `for` loop is inserted, and the cursor is moved to the placeholder `!cursor!` (which is removed). So, you will be ready to fill in the parameters for the `for` loop and jump to the next parameters with *Ctrl+j*.

It probably won't take you long to realize that many programming languages have the same main structures (such as the `for` loop), but they differ just enough to not be able to use the same pattern template. So, let's go back and look at what we already have in our template system, and see if we can make the templates file type aware.

In the previous section, we opened a template file depending on the extension of the file. It looked like this:

```
:autocmd BufNewFile * silent! 0r $VIMHOME/templates/%:e.tpl
```

Let's modify this such that it also loads the appropriate abbreviations for our pattern templates.

To make the code clearer, we also move the functionality out into a function of its own. It could look like the following:

```
function! LoadTemplate(extension)
    silent! :execute '0r $VIMHOME/templates/'. a:extension. '.tpl'
    silent! execute 'source $VIMHOME/templates/'.a:extension.'.patter
ns.tpl'
endfunction
```

And to actually call the function, we change `autocmd` to look like this:

```
:autocmd BufNewFile * silent! call LoadTemplate('%:e')
```

The `LoadTemplate` function looks in the `templates` folder in your `$VIMHOME` for two files, `EXTENSION.tpl` and `EXTENSION.patterns.tpl` where `EXTENSION` is replaced with the extension of the file you are currently opening.

The first file will hold your template for the file type, and the second file will contain the abbreviation commands for all the patterns you have created for this particular file type. If it does not find the file, then `silent!` will make sure that it does not give you an error message, but simply returns nothing to you.

So, now it is up to you to fill in the templates and thereby complete your personal templating system.

 Many template system scripts exist for Vim. Most of them are based on the same concept as described in this chapter. However, they have added even more functionality. I will recommend that you look at mu-template by Gergely Kontra if you would like more templating options than those described here at `http://www.vim.org/scripts/script.php?script_id=222`.

Snippets with the snipMate script

Many template system scripts exist for Vim and most of them are based on the concepts already described. But sometimes you do want Vim to make your life simpler when working with specific file formats. In those cases, you could benefit from using a snippet script. Snippets are like the abbreviations described for templates earlier, but can be a lot more advanced.

If you would like to work with snippets in Vim, I would recommend that you look at the snipMate script at `http://www.vim.org/scripts/script.php?script_id=2540`.

The snipMate script makes it easy for you to define even advanced snippets for your file formats without getting into too much Vim scripting yourself.

If you, for example, want to create a snippet for the `for` loop we made earlier using `iabbrev`, you could do it like this:

```
snippet for
    for (${1:i} = 0; $1 < ${2:count}; $1${3:++}) {
        ${4:/* code */}
    }
```

This text is added to a file placed in `$VIMHOME/snippets` called `FILETYPE.snippet` (where `FILETYPE` is the actual file type; for example, `c` for the C code or `php` for the PHP code).

The first line tells the snippet script that a new snippet is started and that it should be executed when the `for` word is written and the *Tab* key is pressed. (This tells the snippet script to complete the snippet.)

The next line is where the real magic goes on. It actually starts by writing a snippet of code looking like this:

```
for (i = 0; I < count; i++) {
    /* code */
}
```

However, after the snippet is inserted, it places the cursor in the first `i` and goes into the insert mode. That way you can easily change the `i` into another variable name. Now the magic begins because not only is the first `i` changed, but the second one (with `++` after) is also changed automatically. After changing `i` (if needed), you press the *Tab* key and the cursor will jump to `count` and again go into the insert mode. You can now change `count` and press the *Tab* key once again. This time it moves to the `++` and pressing *Tab* again takes you in `/*code */` where you are now ready to fill in the code.

It couldn't be more easy to move between the different variable parts of the snippet.

The snipMate system works by looking for special marks created with `${NUMBER:INITIAL_VALUE}`. The NUMBER in the mark indicates the sequence in which you will jump to it when pressing the *Tab* key. If the NUMBER is 1, then the cursor will be placed there first. If the NUMBER is 3, this is where you will go after pressing the *Tab* key twice, and so on. The INITIAL_VALUE is the text that will be put in the first added snippet before you start changing it. This means that `${1:i}` will put the `i` text and place the cursor on this `i` first.

If you need the same variable in several places, you can simply refer to it by using `$NUMBER`. For example, if you want to add the `i` in several places, you could do it by placing `$1` in other places in the snippet. All places where you put `$1` will initially show up as `i` and will automatically change when you change the first `i` in the snippet.

This is just the basics of how to create snippets for the snipMate plugin. But once you have installed it, you will be able to read more about it in the Vim help system.

You can also find a lot of inspiration in the snippets that are included with the script. Here you will find ready-made snippets for many common file formats such as `.c`, `.php`, `.perl`, `.java`, `.html`, `.tex`, and even Vim scripting.

You can download the snipMate script and read about how to install it directly from the Vim script repository at http://www.vim.org/ scripts/script.php?script_id=2540.

Using tag lists

Tag lists are like a programmer's dictionary. A tag list is actually a file containing all sorts of keywords that can identify parts of a program. It can be function names, variable names, class methods, and so on depending on the programming language that you are using. Tag list files are actually not an output from Vim, but rather an output from one of the several tag list generators. Among these, the best known are as follows:

- Exuberant Ctags: For C, C++, Java, Perl, Python, Vim, Ruby (and 25 others)
- Vtags: For Verilog files
- Jtags: For Java files
- Hdrtags: For C / C++, Asm, Lex / Yacc, LaTeX, Vim, and Maple
- Ptags: For Perl files

Because Ctags is absolutely the most used and the one that supports the most languages, it will be the one we use in the following examples.

We will work with a project written in C that consists of three files:

- `main.c`: The main file containing the main function of the program
- `myfunctions.c`: The source for the functions needed in the program
- `myfunctions.h`: The header file for the functions in `myfunctions.c`

The code in the files is almost done, so let's make a tag file for the files.

We invoke the `ctags` command-line program as follows in the directory where your source files are placed:

```
ctags *.c *.h
```

You will now notice that a new file called `tags` has been created in the directory where you invoked the `ctags` command. This file is your tags file and contains information about all the functions and variables in your code.

The `ctags` program takes a lot of arguments for choosing a programming language and so on. See `ctags-help` for more information.

We need to tell Vim that it should use the `tags` file, which is done by setting the tags setting.

```
:set tags=/path/to/tags
```

Now, Vim knows about the tags and you are ready to use it in your work.

In the main file, we use the functions from the `myfunctions.c` file. Let's say there is a function called `calcValue`, but you are not sure which arguments it takes. Here, it would be nice to see how it is defined and it is here the tags file comes in handy. You simply start typing the function name until the (like this:

```
myvalue = calcValue(
```

Now, place the cursor on the function name, go into the normal mode, and then press *Ctrl-]*. One of the following two things happens:

- There is only one match, and you are moved directly to where the function is defined

- There are multiple possible matches and a list of matches is shown

In the second case, you can select which of the matches in the list you want to jump to. This is nice if you are working with languages where you can overload functions and hence have multiple editions of a function.

After you have looked at the function, you need to go back and actually complete the code that you've started. To do so, simply press *Ctrl+t* and you will be brought back to where you originally came from.

 In Gvim, you can also use the mouse to go to the definition of a keyword. Just hold down the *Ctrl* key while pressing mouse-button 1.

You can view jumping between tags as using a tag stack. When you go to a keyword, you push the tag on the stack and when you go back to the previous place, you pop a tag off the stack.

You can actually see the stack by using the following command:

`:tags`

```
gs
TO tag           FROM line  in file/text
  1 clear_edge_list    71   clear_edge_list();
  1 edge_list          62   edge_list = NULL;
  1 show_operation_failed_dialog   113   show_operation_failed_dialog();

as ENTER or type command to continue
```

The tag in the list that is marked with **>** at the beginning of the line is the tag you are currently at. When using *Ctrl+]* and *Ctrl+t,* you move up and down in the stack, but you can also work the stack with commands:

- `:tag`: Move to the next tag in the stack
- `:pop`: Move to the previous tag in the stack

When you have used a lot of tags and jumped around between them, it might be nice to get a list of the ones you have available. To get such a list, simply use one of the following commands:

- `:tselect`
- `:ptselect`

The first one gives you a list of matching tags, and you can then select the one you want by pressing the number you find at the beginning of the line.

The second command does the same, except that it shows the list in a preview window. If you selected the wrong tag in the list, or just want to see one of the others, then you can move between them with the following commands:

- `:tnext`: Move to the next tag in the list
- `:tprev`: Move to the previous tag in the list

You might not see the strength of the tag lists in this example, but imagine that your project was not just three files, but 1000 files across hundreds of directories. So you suddenly just can't go around remembering where each function is, and you would need a thorough indexing mechanism like tag files.

Easier taglist navigation

On most non-English keyboard layouts, the *]* key is not directly available and you would need to press, for example, *Ctrl+Alt + G + r+9* to execute the *Ctrl+]* tag jump. In those cases, it would be nice to map the commands to more accessible keys. I use the following mappings:

```
:nmap <buffer> <F7> <C-]>
:nmap <buffer> <S-F7> <C-T>
:nmap <buffer> <A-F7> :ptselect<cr>
:nmap <buffer> <F8> :tnext<cr>
:nmap <buffer> <C-F8> :tprev<cr>
```

Now, you can jump back and forth between tags with *F7* and *Ctrl+F7*, get a list of the tags with *Alt+F7*, and go through the used tags with *F8* and *Ctrl+F8*.

Other usages of taglists

Taglists are used by programmers not only for looking up functions and variable definitions, but also for a lot of other interesting things. Just to give you an idea, here's a short list of examples where they are used in Vim scripts:

- `lookupfile.vim`: Hari Krishna Dara has created a script that can use tag lists to find files in a tagged project simply by writing the filename. Find the latest version of the script at:
  `http://www.vim.org/scripts/script.php?script_id=1581.`

- `taglist.vim`: Yegappan Lakshmanan has created the taglist plugin for Vim, which is very popular among programmers. It is a complete source code browser that gives a great overview of the functions, keywords, variables, definitions, and so on in a split window. In Gvim, it can even give you a complete menu with the tags of the project. You can find a lot more information about this plugin at:
  `http://www.vim.org/scripts/script.php?script_id=1581.`

- `ctags.vim`: Gary Johnson and Alexey Marinichev have created a simple yet powerful plugin called `ctags.vim`. It simply shows the name of the function the cursor is currently placed in, that is, in the status bar or window title. The script automatically generates tag files for the currently opened file using the program Exuberant Ctags. Find more information about the script at
  `http://www.vim.org/scripts/script.php?script_id=610.`

- `autoproto.vim`: Jochen Baier has created a very useful script for C programmers. This script shows the prototype of the currently typed in function in a preview window whenever the programmer presses the first (after the function name. Find more information about the script at: `http://www.vim.org/scripts/script.php?script_id=1553`.

 You can read a lot more about tags and how to use them in the Vim help system under `:help tags`.

Using autocompletion

As a Vim user that obeys the philosophy of Vim, you will do anything to minimize the number of key presses because extra keys pressed equals extra time wasted.

So, why type each word to the end when Vim is able to guess what you are typing and automatically complete the word for you?

In Vim, there are multiple ways to autocomplete the words you are typing. Some methods simply complete words you have written once in one of the opened buffers, while others involve analyzing the code you are working on — not just the current file, but the entire source tree.

In the following sections, we will look at three different ways to use autocompletion in Vim:

- Autocompletion with known words
- Autocompletion using a dictionary file
- Context-aware autocompletion with omnicompletion

There will also be some small tricks on how to make it more comfortable to use autocompletion by using well-recognizable key bindings.

Autocompletion with known words

In this recipe, we will look at the simplest type of autocompletion and at the same time the most overlooked type — autocompletion with known words.

No matter what you are writing, you will eventually write the same words repeatedly. In Vim, you can simply type in the first couple of letters of the word and then press *Ctrl+n*.

Example:

You want to write the sentence "I have beautiful flowers in my flower garden".

Since you have no text besides this in the file, you will have to write the entire first part of the text until it looks like "I have beautiful flowers in my f".

Now, you would normally continue typing the word "flower". But as it is already there, you can simply press *Ctrl+n* and the word will expand to "flower".

As your text evolves, you will see that you can start using autocompletion on more and more words.

What *Ctrl+n* actually does is look for a matching word by going forward through the file. If you know that you have just used the word, then it will be faster to use *Ctrl+p* instead because Vim will then search backwards in the file for a matching word. In general, you won't feel the difference unless you are working with really large files, or there are many possible matches.

Autocompletion using dictionary lookup

A neat trick is to find a large dictionary file with all kinds of words in your favorite language, and then load this file into Vim as a dictionary (such files can be easily found on the Internet). To load the file into Vim as a dictionary, simply add it to the dictionary setting with:

```
:set dictionary+=/path/to/dictionary/file/with/words
```

Now, Vim suddenly knows a lot of words beforehand, and you can simply autocomplete using these words. However, something is different. Now the words we use to look in are not the words from one of the open buffers, but keywords from one of the dictionary files available in the dictionary setting. This is why you will need to use another key binding in order to do the completion this time.

```
ctrl-x ctrl-k
```

By pressing *Ctrl+x*, you get into a completion mode and by pressing *Ctrl+k*, you do a lookup for a keyword (remember *k* for keyword) in the dictionaries.

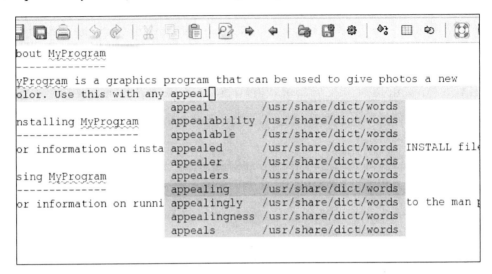

Other completion types are available. Some of them are in the following list:

Ctrl+x plus:

- *Ctrl+l*: Complete whole lines of the text
- *Ctrl+n*: Complete words from the current buffer
- *Ctrl+k*: Complete words from the dictionaries
- *Ctrl+t*: Complete words from the thesaurus (see :help 'thesaurus')
- *Ctrl+i*: Words from the current and included files
- *S*: Spelling the suggestions (Vim 7.0 and newer only)

Others will be described in the next sections.

Omnicompletion

We all have our perfect solution for what should be autocompletable and what shouldn't. In Vim, there was no way to give the user complete control over what to do about completion until version 7.0 came out.

Vim 7.0 introduced a new completion technique called omnicompletion. It gave the user the possibility to define exactly how the functionality of the completion should work—in fact, then, the user would have to write the completion function himself or herself (unless someone else had already done it).

As with the completions mentioned in the previous section, the completion is invoked by typing in some letters and then going into completion mode by pressing *Ctrl+x* followed by *Ctrl+o* to make an omnicompletion.

To add your own completion function, you simply do the following:

```
:set omnifunc=MyCompleteFunction
```

Now, you would just have to create a function called `MyCompleteFunction` that gives you the completions. This setting is only available to the currently active buffer, and you will have to set it for all buffers where you want to use it.

 Setting `omnifunc` is normally done in a file type plugin such that it is bound to a single file type.

So, let's look at an example of how such a function could look like. For instance, assume that you have a file with all your contacts with one name and e-mail address on each line like this:

```
Kim Schulz|kim@schulz.dk
John Doe|john.doe@somedomain.com
Jane Dame|jd@somedomain2.com
Johannes Burg|jobu@somedomain3.net
Kimberly B. Schwartz|kbs@somedomain.com
...
```

Now, you would like to insert an e-mail address by writing a name and doing autocompletion on it. A function for this could look like this:

```
function! CompleteEmails(findstart, base)
    if a:findstart
      " locate the start of the word
      let line = getline('.')
      let start = col('.') - 1
      while start > 0 && line[start - 1] =~ '\a'
        let start -= 1
      endwhile
      return start
    else
      " find contact names matching with "a:base"
      let res = []
      " we read contactlist file and sort the result
      for m in sort(readfile('/home/kim/.vim/contacts.txt'))
        if m =~ '^' . a:base
            let contactinfo = split(m, '|')
```

```
                  " show names in list, but insert email address
                  call add(res, {'word': contactinfo[1],
                          \ 'abbr': contactinfo[0].' <'.contactinfo[1].'>',
                      \ 'icase': 1} )
              endif
          endfor
          return res
      endif
  endfunction
```

The function takes two arguments that are needed for an omnicompletion function. The first time Vim calls the function, it sets the first argument, `findstart`, to 1 (and `base` is empty). This means that this is the first invocation, and that it should find the beginning of the word you have written so far.

Vim then invokes the function again, and this time with `findstart` set to 0 and `base` set to the word you have started autocomplete on. This time the function opens up the contact list file and reads it line by line into a list. It sorts the list such that the list in the completion pop-up is ordered, and then it iterates over the list.

The lines are split at the |, and then the ones that begin with the same letters as the word you completed on are added to a result that the function will return. The function can modify how the pop-up content looks and what it should match on. This is done not by adding the e-mail addresses, but instead by building a dictionary (see `:help Dictionary`) where some specific keys are set. In this case, we use three keywords as follows:

- **Word**: The actual word that should be inserted
- **Abbr**: This word is used instead of **word** in the pop-up list
- **Icase**: If this is a non-zero value, then the matching is case insensitive

Other keywords and their functionality can be found in the help system under this command:

`:help 'omnifunc'`

So, now Vim has a list of words for its popup, or in this case small lines such as:

```
"Kim Schulz <kim@schulz.dk>"
```

Whenever you write some letters such as `ki` and then press *Ctrl+x Ctrl+o*, Vim will show the popup with all the names that start, with `ki`.

```
Using MyProgram
---------------

For information on running and using MyProgram, please refer to the man p

Authors
-------

This progam is written by Kim Schulz k▯
                                        Kim Schulz(kim@schulz.dk)
                                        Kim-Lo Won(kl@business.com.hk)
                                        Kimberly B. Schwartz(kbs@aol.com)
                                        Kimmie Udine(kimmie@udine.cz)
```

To move between the items in the list, you can keep pressing *Ctrl+o* to cycle through the list. Alternatively, you can press *Ctrl+n* to move forward in the list and *Ctrl+p* to go backwards in the list.

All-in-one completion

You might wonder how you will ever be able to remember all these keyboard shortcuts, and why you could not just use the same for all completion types depending on which one you have available. With Vim, you can do this if you want. So, let's look at how we can do this in a way that is easy for you to remember.

Nearly any other editor that supports completion has this functionality mapped to the *Tab* key.

In the help system, you will find a function called `CleverTab()`. The following command will take you right to where you can find the function:

`:help ins-completion`

This function let's you use *Tab* to complete words instead of *Ctrl+n*. It can distinguish between whether it should insert a tab character or do the completion. If you pressed *Tab* at the beginning of the line (indention) or after another whitespace character, it inserts a tab character. In the rest of the cases, it would try to do known word completion.

We take this `CleverTab` function and extend it even further such that it selects the completion method to use from the following prioritized list:

- Omnicompletion
- Dictionary completion
- Known word completion

A function that can do this, could look like the following:

```
function! SuperCleverTab()
    "check if at beginning of line or after a space
    if strpart( getline('.'), 0, col('.')-1 ) =~ '^\s*$'
       return "\<Tab>"
    else
        " do we have omni completion available
        if &omnifunc != ''
           "use omni-completion 1. priority
           return "\<C-X>\<C-O>"
        elseif &dictionary != ''
           " no omni completion, try dictionary completio
           return "\<C-K>"
        else
           "use omni completion or dictionary completion
           "use known-word completion
           return "\<C-N>"
        endif
    endif
endfunction
" bind function to the tab key
inoremap <Tab> <C-R>=SuperCleverTab()<cr>
```

Add the function and the binding to your `vimrc` file, and then you are ready to do completion with your *Tab* key.

You simply have to press the *Tab* key to do your completion, and the function checks to see if it should insert a tab character. If not, then it checks to see if you have a omnicompletion function (in `omnifunc`) available. If this is also not the case, then it looks if there is a dictionary available. If you have no dictionaries available, then it falls back on using the simple known word completion.

Using macro recording

Probably the most overseen production booster when working with monotonic structured text is the ability to record input macros to do them over and over again.

The interface for doing this is extremely simple, but nearly everything can be recorded. So it reveals a very powerful tool.

Let's start by looking at the commands to use:

- qa: Record from now on into register a. Any register can be used, but q is often used for simplicity.
- q: If pressed while recording, the recording is ended.
- @a: Executes the recording in register a (replace with any register).
- @@: Repeats the last executed command.

You can add any number before the @ to repeat the execution of the recording that number of times. For example, 15@a will execute the recording in register a 15 times.

So, let's look at a normal recording session in Vim:

```
qq
command1
command2
....
commandN
q
10@q
```

You might wonder what this can be used for, because when is it exactly that you need to execute a list of commands over and over again. This is best shown with an example.

Imagine you have a large list with information. It could, for example, be a log file from a Unix system that could look something like this:

```
Oct  8 21:23:34 laptopia kernel: ACPI: bus type pci registered
Oct  8 21:23:34 laptopia kernel: PCI: PCI BIOS revision 2.10 entry at
0xe9694
Oct  8 21:23:34 laptopia kernel: Setting up standard PCI resources
Oct  8 21:23:34 laptopia kernel: ACPI: Subsystem revision 20060127
Oct  8 21:23:34 laptopia kernel: ACPI: Interpreter enabled
Oct  8 21:23:34 laptopia kernel: ACPI: Using IOAPIC for interrupt
routing
Oct  8 21:23:34 laptopia kernel: ACPI: PCI Root Bridge [PCI0]
(0000:00)
Oct  8 21:23:34 laptopia kernel: PCI quirk: region 1000-107f claimed
by ICH6
Oct  8 21:23:34 laptopia kernel: PCI quirk: region 1300-133f claimed
by ICH6
Oct  8 21:23:34 laptopia kernel: PCI: Ignoring BAR0-3 of IDE
controller 001:1
Oct  8 21:23:34 laptopia kernel: PCI: Transparent bridge -
0000:00:1e.0
...
```

Now, you want to convert this file into an HTML file where the information is presented in a table with each column of text represented by a table column. You basically want each line to look like this:

```
<tr><td>Oct 8 21:23:34</td><td>laptopia</td><td>kernel:</td><td>ACPI
...</td><tr>
```

You could start editing the file line by line, until you come to the end of the file. But how about just editing one line while recording it, and then playing back the commands on the other lines? The command execution could look like the following, starting with the cursor placed at the beginning of the first line:

Qa	Start recording into register a
i<tr><td>[ESC]	Go into the insert mode, insert first HTML, and go back to the normal mode
/ [CR]	Search forward for whitespace
3n	Advance three whitespace searches forward
xi</td><td>[ESC]	Delete whitespace, go into the insert mode, and add HTML to the normal mode
n	Go to the next whitespace
xi</td><td>[ESC]	Delete whitespace, go into the insert mode, and add HTML to the normal mode
n	Go to the next whitespace
xi</td><td>[ESC]	Delete whitespace, go into the insert mode, and add HTML to the normal mode
A</td></tr>[ESC]	Append the final HTML to the end of the line and go in the normal mode
j^	Advance a line and move to the beginning of it
q	End macro recording

 For all instances of [ESC], press the *Esc* key, and for all instances of [CR], press the *Enter* key.

We now have the full macro recorded and the cursor is placed correctly at the beginning of the next line. This means that we are ready to replay the macro over and over again and the cursor will automatically move to the next line after a replay.

You can play back the recording with @a or you can simply play back the command on each line in the file with 9999@a. All you need now is to add a header and a footer to the file, but that is not really interesting here.

This is just one place where macro recordings can be used and if you think back, you will probably remember situations where you could have optimized your work by using a macro recording.

Using sessions

Have you ever wondered how much information Vim actually holds for you? It holds a wide range of settings and things, some of which are:

- Open files, buffers, windows, and tabs
- Command history
- Points of change in the text
- Selections and undo branches
- Size of windows, splits, and the GUI window
- Place of cursor

The stored information can be split into three different categories:

- The first type of setting is called a **View** and applies to a single window in Vim. A view can be saved and restored such that a window will have the same look and setup every time you use the view.
- The second type of setting is called **Sessions**. It is a collection of views and information about how they are interoperating. Like views, sessions can also be saved for a later retrieval.
- The final type of setting includes all the rest, that is, all the global settings that do not directly apply to any window in Vim. These settings are stored with the session such that they can also be saved / restored.

In the following sections, we will look at how sessions can be used for different tasks during your daily work in Vim.

Simple session usage

When using sessions, the most basic thing to do is to save the currently running session (the default session when no special session is loaded) to a session file such that you can load it again later when you need to. The main command to use is:

```
:mksession FILE
```

Or if you only want to save the current view, use this:

```
:mkview FILE
```

FILE is the name of the file you want to save your session to or view in. If no filename is given, Vim uses a file called Session.vim that it puts in the current work directory.

 If you have previously saved a session with the same filename, you can add a ! after mksession to make it overwrite the file.

When working with views, you can have many different views at the same time. If every view is saved in the current working directory, then it would be filled up with view files. To prevent this, you can tell Vim where it should place the view files with the following command:

```
:set viewdir=$HOME/.vim/views
```

In the previous case, you will set it to store the view files in a directory called views, which is placed in your $HOME/.vim/ directory.

So as an example, we could say that you have three windows open and just before closing Vim you use this:

```
:mksession
```

Then the next time you want to open Vim with the same session, you simply start Vim with the command-line argument -S; for example:

```
vim -S Session.vim
```

Now, Vim will be started with the same settings as when you saved the session. Alternatively, you can open Vim as you normally would and then use the following command to load the session file:

```
:source Session.vim
```

In the case of views, you can instead use the following:

```
:loadview View.vim
```

Loading a session can change the entire layout of the editor, whereas loading a view will only change the layout of the active window.

If you want Vim to remember settings such as cursor placement and folds when moving between multiple folders, you can add the following to your `vimrc` file:

```
set viewdir=$VIMHOME/views/
autocmd BufWinLeave * mkview
autocmd BufWinEnter * silent loadview
```

A view of the buffer is saved whenever you show another buffer in the same window, and it is restored when you show the buffer in the window again.

The trick is to add commands for saving a session when quitting Vim, and restoring the session when opening Vim. This way you can open and close Vim without losing the settings, a list of open files, and so on. You can do this by simply adding the following commands to your `vimrc` file:

```
autocmd VimEnter * call LoadSession()
autocmd VimLeave * call SaveSession()
function! SaveSession()
    execute 'mksession! $HOME/.vim/sessions/session.vim'
endfunction
function! LoadSession()
    if argc() == 0
        execute 'source $HOME/.vim/sessions/session.vim'
    endif
endfunction
```

If you close Vim now, then it saves a session file in `$HOME/.vim/sessions/session.vim`.

Depending on how you open Vim, it either opens the file specified on the command line or reopens the latest session. For example:

- `vim file.txt`: This opens Vim without loading the last session.
- `vim`: This opens Vim with the last session loaded. The previously opened files are reopened.

If you want to store additional settings besides what Vim stores in the session file, you can add an extra session file. This is done by creating a file named like your session file, except that the `.vim` extension is replaced by `x.vim`. For example, `Session.vim` has the extra session file, `Sessionx.vim`. The extra session file should be placed in the same folder as the session file itself. You can then add all the Vim commands you want to in this file, and these will be executed once the session file has been read.

Satisfy your own session needs

It is not always that you want everything saved in your session. Sometimes, it might just be the files you had open that you want to save information about. Other times you want to store every single piece of information you can about a session. Fortunately, Vim gives you a way to set up what you want it to save in a session file.

The setting you should work with is called `sessionoptions` and can be set with:

```
:set sessionoptions=OPTIONS
```

`OPTIONS` is a comma-separated list with one or more of the following options:

blank	Save empty windows
buffers	Save information about all buffers, including the hidden and unloaded buffers
curdir	Save information about the current work directory
folds	Save information about the folds in the buffer contents
globals	Save information about global variables; only variables starting with an uppercase letter and of the type String or Number will be saved
help	Save the help window
localoptions	Save information about local options and mappings you have created for a single window
options	Save all options, both local and global
resize	Save information about the size of the UI window (lines and columns)
sesdir	If set, the current directory is the place where the session file is saved (cannot be used when curdir is also set)
slash	Change the backslashes in all paths to slashes (make Windows paths Unix compatible)
tabpages	Save information about all tab pages and not only the active one, which is the default without this option
unix	Use Unix line endings, even on Windows system
winpos	Save information on where the UI Window was placed on the screen
winsize	Save the size of all open windows.

The options marked with bold are the ones Vim has turned on as per default. Instead of setting the entire list of options, whenever you want to add or remove a single one, you can instead use the += and -= operators. If you, for example, have the default options but would like to have winpos added to the options and also have folds removed, then simply do this:

```
:set sessionoptions+=winpos
```

```
:set sessionoptions-=folds
```

You can see which options you have in your sessions options using:

```
:echo &sessionoptions
```

You can, in fact, see any of the settings in Vim by simply using the :echo and adding an & in front of the setting's name—for example, :echo &somesetting.

Sessions as a project manager

You might sometimes want to use session files as a sort of primitive project file with information about some project you are working on. So, when working on a project and having a lot of files and windows open, you simply use:

```
mksession!
```

This command would help you save the current session to the Session.vim file in the folder that you are working from. It would then be ideal if Vim automatically loaded the session for the project if there was a project file (Session.vim). So, why not make this possible? Simply add the following to your vimrc file:

```
silent source! Session.vim
```

Now, if there is a Session.vim file in the folder where you start Vim, then it will load it. So, as long as you keep the session file in the project directory, you can easily reload the project in Vim over and over again—just remember to save the the session again if you open new files or change the windows / buffers.

This is just a simple way of using sessions as a project manager, but it can be made a lot more advanced. Wenzhi Liang has created a practical script that adds a Projects menu item to Gvim. In this menu, it is possible to save the current session as a named project. Later, you can restore the project (which is now available directly in the menu) or you can switch between projects with a single click of a menu item. If you don't need a project anymore, then you can simply choose to delete it through the menu.

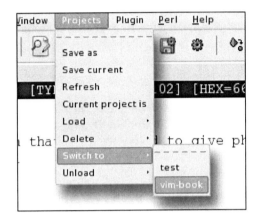

You can find the latest version of the script and read more about it on this home page at:

`http://www.vim.org/scripts/script.php?script_id=279`

The script demands that you have both Perl and Bash installed on your computer.

Registers and undo branching

You might know the feeling when you delete or cut something from your text, and realize later that you needed that text elsewhere. If you have already copied / cut another piece of text, then the old text is gone because the clipboard normally has room only for one piece of text—but not in Vim.

In Vim, you have two tools that can help when you modify your text and need to keep a track of deleted / copied text or changes to the text in general:

- Registers: Registers is sort of an advanced clipboard with multiple buffers for storing your clippings, deleted, and copied text.

- Undo branching: Undo branching is a simple form of version control built into Vim. It gives you the possibility to roll back the changes to a file until a certain time or a certain number of changes. If you later regret undoing some changes, you can go back and find an undo branch containing those exact changes.

The next two sections will tell you more about how to use both registers and undo branching in your daily work. After reading them, you will easily see why these tools are very strong tools and how they can help you in your daily work in Vim.

Using registers

In many programs and operating systems, you only have access to a single clipboard for the text you cut or copy. This is not the case with Vim because here you have access to not one, not two, but nine different clipboards, or register types as they are called.

Some of the register types overlay each other's working area, while others have a very unique purpose. You can use the registers in connection with a range of commands and movements such as yank, delete, and paste. The registers are all named with " in front of the name, for example "x. So, let's look at how to use a register. Let's just say that we use the register called "x in the examples. What x actually should be will be explained later.

To store a piece of text that you want to copy into a register, you can use the normal y for the yank, except that you start out by telling it where to yank it to:

"x y (or "x yy if you want to copy the entire line).

Same is the case when cutting text with the x command:

"x x

Or, when deleting text with the d command:

"x d

So, now you have the text stored in the register "x and you want to paste it again. You can simply use the P (after cursor) and p (before cursor) commands to paste the text and start out by telling Vim which register to paste:

"x p or "x P

If you have forgotten which register you used, then you can simply type in this command:

```
:registers
```

So, now you know how to use the registers with the basic commands in Vim, and it is time to look a bit further at the different register types. The following sections describe each of the nine types of registers.

The unnamed register

The unnamed register is called so because it is accessed through `""`, hence resembling the empty string or no name. Vim automatically fills this register whenever some text is yanked with `y` or deleted with one of the following commands: `d` (delete), `c` (delete and go into insert mode), `s` (substitute), or `x` (cut). What this register does is point to the last used register, which also means that it will work even if you use a specific register when deleting / yanking a text. For example, `"xdd` will fill both the `x` register and the unnamed register.

If you paste some text with `p` or `P` without specifying any register, then it actually gets the text it pastes from the unnamed register.

The small delete register

Whenever you delete less than one line of text, Vim will move it into a very specific register—the small delete register (`"-`). The only exception to this case is when you specify another register to use.

The numbered registers

The numbered registers are named `"0`, `"1`, `"2`, and so on up to `"9`. They can be split into two types. The first type is register `"0`, which always contains the last deleted (`d` or `x`) / changed (`c`) text. When you delete or change something new, then register `"0` is overwritten with the new text.

Like register `"0`, register `"1` also contains the last changed / deleted text. There is, however, the difference that register `"1` will not be updated if another register is specified, or if the text is less than one-line long (the small delete register is then used). For compatibility with vi, there is an exception where register `"1` is used no matter what the length is. This is if one of the following movement commands is used in your change / delete: `%`, `(`, `)`, `{`, `}`, `` ` ``, `/`, `?`, `n`, `N`.

Unlike register `"0`, the contents of register `"1` are not deleted whenever a new text is added. Instead, it is moved to register `"2`. If register `"2` was already full, then this text is moved to register `"3` first, and so on until register `"9`. The contents of register `"9` will be overwritten whenever any new content is added. This way the registers from `"1` to `"9` can function as a delete / change history such that you can get access to earlier deleted text even if you have deleted new text more recently.

The named registers

There are two types of named registers — `"a` to `"z` and `"A` to `"Z`.

If you use the lowercase registers such as `"a`, then they work like a normal register that you can copy deleted or changed data into. When a new text is added to a register, the old contents are discarded.

If you instead use the uppercase registers (for example, `"A`) then the previous content of the register is not deleted, but the new text is instead appended to the register.

 If you add the value `'>'` to your `coptions`, then the appended text in uppercase registers is split by a new line: `:set coptions+='>'`.

Since you have complete control over the named registers, they are most likely the type of registers you will get familiar with first.

The read-only registers

There are four different read-only registers. What makes these registers so special is that only Vim has access to them. You only have access to pasting them with the normal P, p, or :put commands. The contents of the read-only registers are quite different:

- `"%`: This register always contains the name of the file in the currently active buffer.
- `"#`: This register always contains the name of the previous file in the currently active buffer, also called the alternate file.
- `".`: This register always contains the last inserted text. Therefore, you will be able to repeat the last inserted text by executing the normal mode command `".P`.

- " :: This register contains the command you last executed on the command line. If you repeat a command from the history, then this register will not be overwritten with the command. You will have to write at least one character of the command in order to get it stored in the register.

The selection and drop registers

This register type consists of three registers: " *, " +, and " ~. The registers are used to store and retrieve the text you have selected in Gvim. The " * register actually accesses the clipboard of your windowing system. If you use Microsoft Windows, then you wont feel any difference between using " * and " +. On Linux, however, there is a difference between the two registers because the Clipboard in **X11** (the windowing system) has not just one selection register, but three. The contents of the " + register are any text you have selected. They are typically inserted by pressing the middle button on the mouse. However, the contents of the " * register are altered only if you actually tell Vim to yank the text.

These registers can be accessed from any GUI application, and are part of the normal copy-paste procedure you know from your daily work.

The last register in this group is the drop register " ~. This register contains the last selection that has been dropped into Vim. So, if you select some text in another application and drag it to your Gvim window to drop it there, then " ~ register will contain this text.

The black hole register

As the name of this register indicates, this register works like a black hole— everything that goes into it never comes out again. This register is used if you want to completely delete some text and don't even want a record of it in any register. The black hole register is " - and an example of using it is " -x or " -dd. If you try to read out the text you have just written to this register, you will see that no matter what you do, it doesn't return anything.

Search pattern register

Whenever you do a search with the / command, the pattern you are searching for is automatically added to the search pattern register. The register name " / is easy to remember because it resembles the search command / and just has the quotes added to show that it is, in fact, a register. Vim uses this register when you have `hlsearch` (highlight search pattern) turned on. You can use this to your advantage because as this is a register, you can just change its contents to get `hlsearch` to highlight something different. To change the contents of the register without doing a new search, you can simply use:

```
:let "/ = PATTERN
```

Here, PATTERN is what you want hlsearch to highlight.

The expression register

The expression register is the last register type in Vim. Calling it a register is, however, not exactly accurate because it does not store text as the normal registers do. You cannot even write to it. Instead, it opens up the possibility to get access to the command line, execute an expression, and then get the result returned as if it were already stored in the register.

You get access to the expression register by simply typing its name "=. After pressing the equal sign, the cursor will be moved to the command line. You can see that you are working inside the expression register if there is an equal sign as the first character on the command line. You can now write the expression you want the result of and then end by pressing the *Return* key, or alternatively press the *Esc* key to return without executing the expression. If you press the *Return* key without writing any expression, then Vim will find the latest expression executed and use this instead. The expression needs to be valid and should return a string. If the result of the expression is a number, then Vim automatically converts it into a string. However, if you are unsure what type the result has, then simply use the string() function to convert the result before returning it.

 Look at :help expression to see how to put together a valid Vim expression.

Using undo branching

We all know the feature where we can undo changes that we have done to a text. Normally you would just press the undo button in the tool bar or use the right key combination and then the last change to the text would be reverted.

Vim has taken it a bit further and added the concept of branching to this.

In this recipe, we will look at just what undo branching is and how it can help you in your work.

Let's start by defining what an undo branch is in Vim. Let's say that you have a file where you have applied a range of changes. At some point, you realize that the last four changes were wrong and that you do not need them at all. You execute undo (u in the normal mode) four times in a row (or press 4u) as you normally would, and then the last four changes are gone. At this point, you have used undo as you would in any other editor. Now you see that you need to make an extra change to the file — let's say that you needed to correct a spelling error — and you add that also.

Normally, your four undo changes would be gone — but not in Vim.

When you reverted the four changes and added the new changes, you actually added another branch to your undo branch tree. The tree looks like this:

edit(reverted)-edit(reverted)-edit(reverted)-edit(reverted)

/

edit-edit-edit-edit — edit (spelling corretion)

In one branch you have the four changes you reverted, and in the other branch you have your most recent change (the spelling correction). If you just keep adding / editing your text from now on, you would only have these two branches in your undo tree. But you could also add other branches to your undo branch tree simply by doing another undo followed by another edit. In the end, you could end up with quite a branch-filled tree with all the undo and edit actions you have done.

At this point, it might be nice to get an overview of the branches you currently have. This is done with the following command:

`:undolist`

This will get you a list that shows you three pieces of information about each branch — the change number (used to identify a branch), the number of changes in a branch, and the time of the branch creation. It could look like this:

```
number changes    time ~
  6        5       12:12:11
  11       8       14:01:15
```

If you want to go to one of the specific change numbers, then simply use:

`:undo N`

Here N is the change number.

You could also move backwards in the list of changes using the following normal mode command:

g- (Use g+ if you want to move forward instead.)

So, what is the difference between using g- and u to go back through the changes? Let's visualize it with an example.

Write the following text in Vim:

```
My name is Jim
```

Then go to the J and press x three times to delete the name Jim. You now have:

```
My name is Jim
My name is im
My name is m
My name is
```

Now you realize that your name is Jimmy, so you undo the change:

```
My name is m
My name is im
My name is Jim
```

You now have one branch with the deletion of the name Jim. Now, change the name to Jimmy:

```
My name is Jimm
My name is Jimmy
```

But wait! Your name is actually Kim and not Jimmy. Jim was close to Kim, so let's undo back to this place using u and change J to K.

```
My name is Jimm
My name is Jim
My name is im
My name is Kim
```

Another branch was added when you were undoing the change from Jim to Jimmy.

Now, let's go back through the changes with multiple executions of g-:

```
My name is Kim
My name is im
```

(Vim changes to new branch after bracket)

```
My name is Jim
My name is Jimm
My name is Jimmy
```

(Vim changes to new branch after bracket)

```
My name is
My name is m
My name is im
My name is Jim
```

Now, let's compare this to using u for undoing the changes:

```
My name is Kim
My name is im
My name is Jim
My name is Jimm
My name is Jimmy
My name is Jim
```

As you can see, the u command only takes you directly through the changes that are not in branches, whereas g- takes you through every single change in every branch.

So basically, undo branches can give you access to any text state your file content has had.

Instead of going step-by-step through the changes in all the branches, you could instead jump a time slice back in your "edit time". For this, Vim has two commands that jump different time slices back and forth in the undo history depending on the argument. The commands are like this:

`:earlier Ns`

`:earlier Nm`

`:earlier Nh`

`:later Ns`

`:later Nm`

`:later Nh`

Here N is the number of seconds (s), minutes (m), or hours (h) you want to jump back / forward in time. If you use the :undolist function, then you can see the time of the changes and from this you can calculate how far back / forward to jump.

It might take some time to get used to having the undo branches, but when you have gotten used to them, they will help you a lot in your work.

Folding

Often, when you work with large files, especially code, it can be hard to get a good overview. In Vim, there is a special feature that helps you get around this—folding text blocks into folds. In this recipe, we will look at how to use folds to make your code easier to overview.

A fold is a way of *folding* a range of lines (for example, a function scope) into one single line without losing the contents. An example could be the following code:

```
function myFunction(){
    var a = 1;
    var b = 0;
    var c = a+b;
    return c;
}
```

If this is folded, then it could be set to look like this:

```
+-- 6 lines: function myFunction(){ ------------------------------
```

In this case, the folding follows the syntax of the code and uses the { } to figure out where to do the folding. Besides using syntax, Vim can also do folding according to the following:

- Manual fold marks: Manually mark fold (see `:help fold-manual`)
- Indent folds: Use indentation as fold indication (see `:help fold-indent`)
- Expression folds: Use an expression to find folds (see `:help fold-expr`)
- Syntax folds: Use syntax as a fold indication (see `:help fold-syntax`)
- Diff folds: Fold unchanged text (see `:help fold-diff`)
- Marker folds: Insert markers in the text as a fold indication (see `:help fold-marker`)

Which type of fold indication should be used depends on the type of the text you are working on, and also what you find to be the best for you.

So, let's look at how you actually do the folding. The first thing to do is to actually activate the functionality:

```
:set foldenable
```

Now, Vim knows that it should watch out for folding commands when in the normal mode. There is a range of commands you can use to open and close folds, but the primary ones are as follows:

- `zc`: Close a fold
- `zo`: Open a fold
- `zM`: Close all folds
- `zR`: Open all folds

If we take the syntax folding method as an example, then you just need to place the cursor somewhere in the area you want to fold (for example, inside a function scope) and then you go into the normal mode and press `zc` to close the fold. Now you will see the function get folded into a single line. In the following figure, you can see both the folded and the unfolded code mixed together:

```
79 void show_save_graph_as_dialog( GtkMenuItem* menu_item, gpointer user_data ){
80     char* filename_selected;
81     gint response;
82     GtkWidget* save_graph_as_dialog = glade_xml_get_widget( xml, "save_graph_as_dialog" );
83     response = gtk_dialog_run( (GtkDialog*) save_graph_as_dialog );
84     gtk_widget_hide( save_graph_as_dialog );
85
86 -- if( GTK_RESPONSE_OK == response ){...6 Lines... }
92 }
93
94 +void show_save_rendering_dialog( GtkWidget* widget, gpointer user_data ){...16 Lines...}
110
111 void show_render_window( GtkWidget* widget, gpointer user_data ){
112     GtkWidget* render_win;
113     GtkWidget* render_drawing_area;
```

 If you don't want to remember commands for both the opening and the closing folds, then simply bind a key to toggle a fold open or closed. This could be, for example, space: `:nnoremap <space> za`.

If you find that the design of the folded line is not giving you the information you need, then you can change it easily. Simply change the value of the `foldtext` option to point to another function that returns the line you want:

```
:set foldtext=MyFoldFunction()
```

The function could look like the following:

```
function! MyFoldFunction()
```

```
let line = getline(v:foldstart)
" cleanup unwanted things in first line
let sub = substitute(line, '/\*\|\*/\|^\s+', '', 'g')
" calculate lines in folded text
let lines = v:foldend - v:foldstart + 1
return  v:folddashes.sub.'...'.lines.' Lines...'.getline(v:foldend)
```

This function changes your folded line to look like this:

```
+--function myFunction(){...6 Lines...}--------------------------
```

You can see that the function used three different variables whose names start with
v:. These are variables set by Vim and contain:

- v:foldstart: Line number of first line in fold
- v:foldend: Line number of last line in fold
- v:folddashes: Contains a dash (-) for each level of folding a fold

The last variable gives a fast indication of how many levels down are you in the
folding tree. Suppose you have this:

```
if (x != y){
    if (y !=x){
        print "x not y";
        }
}
```

Then v:folddashes in the innermost if will contain "--" (second level), but in the
outermost if it will contain "-" (first level).

The dashes at the end of the fold line are automatically added. If you want a different
character instead of a dash, then this can also be changed. If you, for example, want
to change it to equal sign (=) instead of dashes, then simply use this:

`:set fillchars=fold:=`

You might wonder why dashes, but there is actually quite an obvious explanation.
Vim has another fold setting called foldcolumn that tells it how many columns to
the left of the text it should use for fold information. It actually uses the columns to
draw an ASCII fold tree where the dashes in the folds are the leaves. For example:

```
| some text
+- a first level fold -------------------------------
|
X  beginning of open fold.
2  indication of fold level
2    - do -
```

```
- open fold beginning level 1
+-- a second level fold.
| more text
| more text
```

As you can see, it basically draws a tree which looks like this:

```
|
+-
|
+--
|
+-
+--
```

To set how wide the tree should be, simply use:

`:set foldcolumn=N`

Here, N is a number between 0 and 12. A value of 1 or 2 is recommended only if you have a few levels of folds; otherwise you should use 3-5.

 You can execute a command on all folds that are either open or closed:

- `:folddoopen` cmd: Execute cmd on all lines that are not in a closed fold

- `:folddoclose` cmd: Execute cmd on all lines in the closed folds

Simple text file outlining

Sometimes when you write a simple text file in Vim and you suddenly realize that it has grown from simple to long and chaotic, you could really use a good way to outline the text. In this recipe, we look at how to use folding in Vim to do just that, especially if you think quite a bit about how you structure your text.

Let's say you have a text like this:

```
Chapter 1
Section 1 - Vim help
here is some text about the vim help system.
Section 2 - vim scripts
this section contains  info about vim scripts.
```

Now you would like to fold the text such that only the section headers are shown. If you use manual folding (`:set foldmethod=manual`), this is quite simple. You simply need to mark all lines in a section (including header line) and then press *Z + F*. Now you have created a fold containing those lines. If you start from the outside and go inwards, then you can have say `Chapter 1` as the first level, and each section as fold level 2. If you close the section folds, it would look like this:

```
-Chapter 1
+Section 1 - Vim help   (2)
+Section 2 - vim scripts   (4)
```

> To make it look exactly as the previous example, you will need the following settings:
>
> `:set foldcolumn=1`
>
> `:set fillchars=fold:\   "there is a space after the \`
>
> `:set foldtext=getline(v:foldstart).'   ('.v:foldstart.')'`

As you can see, this looks a lot like the table of contents in a book, but the difference is that this is just a simple text file. As long as you add new text to the sections by appending it to the previous lines (newlines are okay), Vim will still know that your added text is part of the fold.

If you later want to delete a fold, then you simply mark the text again in the visual mode and then press *Z + D*.

If you want to use a different formatting of your text (for example, having = = around the section headers), you can do that—as long as you mark your own folding areas, then you won't feel a difference.

Using vimdiff to track the changes

Sometimes you have multiple versions of the same file—maybe they are the same and maybe they are not. On Unix systems, there has been a program called `diff` available for many years (first release in 1974), but on other operating systems you most likely do not have this. This program gives the user an output that shows the differences between two files. Vim has a solution for you that gives this functionality and even presents it in an easy-to-overview format, `vimdiff`. This recipe will show you how to use Vim to get an overview of changes to your file compared to other versions of the same file.

`vimdiff` is actually a built-in `diff` program, which uses colors to show the differences between two files (shown in two windows in Vim split vertically or horizontally). The following figure shows what a `vimdiff` session could look like:

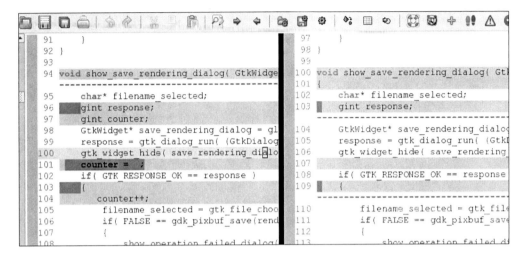

There are several different ways to activate `vimdiff`. On many systems, a program shortcut is made that is called `vimdiff`. In those cases, you can simply use:

```
vimdiff file1 file2
```

This is actually a shortcut for writing this:

```
vim -d file1 file2
```

You will need to supply at least two versions of the file, but up to four versions of the file are supported.

If you are already in an open Vim session, then you can also activate the `diff` mode in Vim. To do so, you will have to use one of the following commands:

- `:diffsplit filename`: Split the window horizontally and show the `filename` file in both of the windows. All diff-specific settings are set for both windows.

- `:vert diffsplit filename`: Split the window vertically and show the `filename` file in both of the windows. All diff-specific settings are set for both windows.

- `:diffthis`: Add the current window to the existing set of diff-enabled windows. This could be used if you want to `diff` a file again with yet another version.

An example could be to see which changes you have made to the currently active file since the last time Vim saved a backup of the file (those copies of the files saved with ~ after the name). If you are working on a file called main.c, then you could at any time save the file and then execute the following command:

:vert diffsplit main.c~

Now the current window is split vertically into two, and you will be able to see the changes you have made to the file marked with colors (depending on your color theme).

- Maybe it wasn't actually you who made the changes to one of the versions of the file and maybe another developer just sent you a patch for your file. But don't worry, Vim can still give you a nice `diff` view of the changes the patch makes to your version of the file. Simply open your version of the file and then with it in the active window, execute this command `:vert diffpatch patchfile` or just `:diffpatch patchfile`.

Here, `patchfile` is the patch the other developer sent you. Now Vim will open another window with your file, and then apply the patch to it. Next, it will set up all the `diff` settings for the windows such that the changes are colored.

Navigation in vimdiff

Navigation in the `vimdiff` windows is a bit different than in the normal Vim windows.

When, for instance, you scroll through the file in one of the windows in the `diff` split, you will see that the other part of the `diff` windows is also scrolled. In fact, the windows follow each other in a way such that the current line in one window is the same line (if available) as in the other window. This is called `scrollbind`:

- It can be turned on using:

  `:set scrollbind`

- It can be turned off using:

  `:set noscrollbind`

You can edit the files in the `diff` windows and you will see that the diff colors are updated accordingly; if not, then try executing the following command:

`:diffupdate`

When you are in one of the `diff` windows, you might want to jump fast between changes done to the file. This is done with the following commands in the normal mode:

- `[c`: Go to start of the previous change
- `]c`: Go to start of the next change

This way you can navigate between relevant areas in a file and get a good idea of which changes have been made to the file.

When the cursor is placed in one of the changes that you can see in the `vimdiff` window, you might realize that this change is also needed in the other version of the file. So now you could copy the lines in the change and insert them into the other file in the right place. But why invest time in this when Vim has made it a lot easier for you? Vim has a function that simply puts the change from one file version into the correct place in another version of the same file. The command is this:

`:diffput`

This command should be executed when the cursor is placed in the change you want to move to the other file version. If, on the other hand, you are in the file without the change, then you could either move to the other file and then put the change back into the first file; or use the Vim way of doing it with the following command:

`:diffget`

Alternatively, you can use `do` in the normal mode for getting a change and `dp` for putting a change.

Read more about vimdiff in `:help vimdiff`.

Using diff to track changes

From the previous section, we know how to use `vimdiff` to make a `diff` of different versions of the same file. But what if you really just want to know what you have changed in the current buffer before saving it? This recipe gives you a little trick to check for changes between the version of the file you have on your hard drive and the one you have in the buffer. In other words, it will show you what you have changed in the buffer since the last time you saved.

What you have to do is to add the following function to your `vimrc` file:

```
function! DiffWithFileFromDisk()
  let filename=expand('%')
  let diffname = filename.'.fileFromBuffer'
  exec 'saveas! '.diffname
  diffthis
  vsplit
  exec 'edit '.filename
  diffthis
endfunction
```

The function stores a temporary copy of the file you have in the current buffer (including latest changes), and then it `diffs` this file against the version of the file you have on your hard drive.

To call the function, use the following command:

:call DiffWithFileFromDisk()

Or, if you want to access it faster, then you can bind a key to the command like this:

:nmap <F7> :call DiffWithFileFromDisk()<cr>

This binds the *F7* key to the function call, and then you just have to go into the normal mode and press *F7* to see the changes marked in the `diff` mode.

Now, you can quickly and easily go through the changes that you have made to the file and check if all of them are important.

Open files anywhere

System administrators and web developers have one thing in common, which can be a big point of annoyance for both of them if they don't have an easy way to get around it. They both work with files that are most often placed on remote servers of some sort.

The system administrator mostly gets around the problem by logging in on the remote server through, for example, an **SSH (secure shell)** connection, and then edits the configuration files and so on directly on the server.

The web developer, on the other hand, gets around the problem by uploading and downloading the files between the remote computer and his or her local computer using an FTP client or by using systems such as Webdav.

But what if it didn't have to be that way? What if they could simply edit the files on the remote system directly from their local system? In Vim, this is possible without any further extensions besides what normally comes with it. Vim has a system called **netrw** (for net read / write), which comes in handy whenever you want to work with files on remote servers. Let's get right to it and start with an example.

Imagine a web developer, John, who has his home page placed on a remote system called `remote.server.com`. He wants to edit his `index.html` file, which resides in the `public_html/` directory in his home directory on the server. In this case, the web developer could simply open the file in Vim like this:

```
vim ftp://john@remote.server.com/public_html/index.html
```

Vim recognizes that it needs to use the FTP protocol and then connects to the FTP server on `remote.server.com` using `john` as the username. If a password is needed to log in, then Vim will prompt you for it. Vim transfers a temporary copy of the file to the local machine and then lets you edit it like any other file. The only difference is that whenever you save the file, it is saved onto the remote server also.

If he had already opened Vim, then John could instead open the site with one of the following commands:

```
:Nread ftp://john@remote.server.com/public_html/index.html
```

```
:Nread remote.server.com john PASSWORD public_html/index.html
```

Change `PASSWORD` to be the password you want to use for the FTP server. Besides reading a file from a remote server, you can also open a local file and write it to the remote server, or go about opening a file on one remote server and save it onto another. The command for writing a file to a remote FTP server is:

```
:Nwrite ftp://user@server/path/to/filename
```

```
:Nwrite server user password path/filename
```

> The format of the arguments from `:Nread` and `:Nwrite` can differ from protocol to protocol. Use `:Nread ?` and `:Nwrite ?` to get help on the exact syntax.

Besides the FTP protocol, Vim supports many other protocols such as:

- SCP
- SFTP
- RCP
- HTTP (read-only)
- DAV

- rsync (read-only)
- fetch (read-only)

To use these, you simply change the `ftp` part of the previous example to one of the other protocol names (in lowercase).

There is, however, a catch. Vim is dependent on external command-line programs in order to use the different protocols. On Linux systems, most of these programs are available by default. But on Mircosoft Windows, only FTP is available. You can find a list of the external programs that Vim uses as a default and an explanation of how to change them in the help system:

```
:help netrw-externapp
```

Besides reading and writing files, Vim is also able to give you a directory listing such that you can use it for finding the right remote files to edit. You just have to point your `:Nread` to a directory instead of a file. For example:

```
:Nread scp://user@server/some/directory/
```

You can select any file in the directory listing and it will then be opened in Vim as if it was a local file.

 If you use Linux, then you can store usernames and passwords for remote sites in a `.netrc` file in your home directory. See `:help netrw-netrc` for more information.

Faster remote file editing

So now you have learned how to work with remote files directly, and you will at some point get into a situation where you have several remote files open at the same time. But then you suddenly hit an annoying situation—you need to log in every time you move to another buffer with, for example, `:bufferprev` and `:buffernext`.

As a default, Vim tries to reload the contents of a buffer whenever it is shown in a window. This means that if the file in the buffer is a remote file, then Vim will need to log in again in order to check if the file should be reloaded.

But is that actually necessary? If you can live with the fact that a remote file can be edited by another person while you are editing it remotely (without you being notified about it), you can trick Vim into not reloading the file.

Each buffer has a set of options that tells Vim what to do with the particular buffer in different situations. One of the options is `bufhidden`, which tells Vim what to do when a buffer is hidden (not shown in a window). This option is normally not set to anything, but if you set it to `hide`, then you tell Vim to just hide the buffer when it is not in a window, and then just show it again when you show it again in a window. Simply, add the following to your `vimrc` file:

```
:set bufhidden=hide
```

And that's basically it. Now you won't have to re-log in whenever you switch buffer and will feel just as if you were editing a local file.

Summary

In this chapter, we have been looking at how to improve our daily work in Vim. Many approaches have been touched, each with a specific area to optimize.

We started out by looking at how to use templates to minimize the amount of text to enter. The first time, our templates were simple ones that used the abbreviation functionality in Vim to emulate the insertion of a template. Next, we improved on our template system by creating template files for specific file types and thereby made it possible to insert an entire skeleton into a programming file. Finally, we looked at how to use the snipMate script to make advanced snippets for any file format.

After the templates, we moved on and looked at another way to minimize the word entry time—autocompletion. Different approaches for autocompletion were discussed and a function was proposed for binding all autocompletion to a single key—*Tab*.

By recording a list of commands, you can get around the boring task of entering the same commands over and over again. We looked at how to do Vim macro recording and use this to change a simple text file into a fine HTML file in a matter of minutes.

Next up was Vim sessions and how to use it for everything from saving the look of a window to using sessions as a full-fledged project manager.

With registers, you have the possibility to use not one, not two, but nine different registers / clipboards.

Using the folding of the text, you can get a better overview of a file because every unnecessary part is hidden in a fold. You can even use folding for creating simple outlines of a text file.

So now the file is changed, but what has actually been touched in the file? We looked at how to use the built-in `diff` functionality in Vim. This gives you an improved overview of where and what you have changed in the active files, and you can even undo or add new changes while still maintaining the good `diff` overview.

Working with files on the local machine is one thing, and working on remote files is another. In Vim, it is possible to work in and navigate remote files directly. This way you won't know whether the file is local or remote.

After reading this chapter and playing around with the recipes, you should soon feel how your workday has improved.

Now, you are ready to move on to the next chapter where we will look at how to use the formatting options of Vim to easily format your text and code.

5
Advanced Formatting

Often, the simplest modification to a text or a piece of code is what changes it from being obscure to being easily readable. In this chapter, we will look at some of the simple tricks you can use to format the text you are working on—no matter whether it is plain text or code.

This chapter will have recipes in three categories:

- Text formatting
- Code formatting
- Using external formatter programs

After reading this chapter, you should have a good idea about what is possible and what is not when it comes to text formatting in Vim.

Formatting text

Even though most people prefer graphical word processors such as Microsoft Word or OpenOffice Writer when they want to write plain text, there are still times where an editor such as Vim will do it just as well. In the following sections, we will look at how to use the strengths of Vim when formatting normal text.

Putting text into paragraphs

This recipe is probably one of the simplest in this book, but at the same time one of the most versatile when it comes to formatting plain text. Imagine that you are writing a piece of text, and just keep on writing without bothering about changing lines or formatting the text. At some point, you might end up with one or more very long lines and conclude that you should start formatting the text. At this point, you have two choices:

- Go through the text and add the formatting manually
- Use the strength of Vim and format the entire paragraph with one command

Obviously, the latter option is the fastest one and at the same time the formatting will be consistent. So, let's look at which command to use for this:

```
gqap
```

This command is actually a combination of a command and a movement, specifically:

- `gq`: Format everything the next movement moves over
- `ap`: "A paragraph" moves over the current paragraph

In other words, the command created by combining `gq` and `ap` simply tells Vim to move over the current paragraph and format it. A paragraph is defined as all the lines between two empty lines. In order to change to another paragraph, you simply add an empty line.

The formatting that Vim adds to the text is basically nice line breaks such that the lines are not longer than a specific length (split correctly between words).

The text formatting width is defined in the Vim option `textwidth` such that if you want a maximum of 80 characters on each line, then you would need to have the following in your `vimrc` file:

```
:set textwidth=80
```

If the option is set to `0`, then Vim sets it to the width of the window—but never more than the number of characters defined in the `textwidth` setting.

You can set how Vim formats a paragraph by setting the Vim option called `formatoptions`. See `:help 'formatoptions'` and `:help 'fo-table'` for more information on how to set this option.

`gq` can be used together with any movement command and after performing the formatting, it will place the cursor where it ends (typically at the end of the last line in that particular area). If, instead, you want the cursor to go back to the place where it originally was before executing the command, then simply change `gq` to `gw`. If you have the cursor placed at the beginning of the first line and do `gwap`, then the cursor will remain there even though the paragraph is formatted.

You can repeat the formatting multiple times by prepending the command with the number of times it should be repeated, for example, `5gqap` will format the current and the next four paragraphs. If you want to format all the paragraphs in a file, you can do it with the `1gqG` command.

This formatting command does not only apply to plain text, but also to any other type of content and you can decide what formatting it should apply.

You can set any function to be the `formatter` for any given file format, simply by setting it in the Vim option called `formatexpr`. If, for instance, you work with a C source code file, you should simply have the following in your `vimrc` file:

```
:set formatexpr=c#Formatter()
```

This tells Vim that when it opens a file of type C, it should use the function called `Formatter()` in the autoloaded file for the C file type.

 Autoloaded files can be found in your `VIMHOME` in a folder called `autoload`. Files are named as the file type and appended with `.vim`. For example, `VIMHOME/autoload/c.vim` for the C file type.

A formatting function has three variables that you can use to find the text you have told it to format:

- `v:num`: The line number of the first line to format
- `v:count`: The number of lines to format
- `v:char`: This variable holds a character that is going to be inserted, it can be empty

A simple formatting function could look like this:

```
function! MyFormatter()
    let first = v:num
```

```
    let last = v:num + v:count
    while(first<=last)
        call setline(first, '> '. getline(first))
        let first = first+1
    endwhile
endfunction
```

This formatting function takes all the lines it is set to work on, and then prepends the lines with > like quoted text in e-mails.

The previously mentioned formatting function is a very simple one. If it is a bit more advanced, the complexity of the function rises quite fast. This is why the number of publicly available formatting functions is limited to a very few (that are created for very specific purposes).

Aligning text

One of the most basic formatting options in most word processors is the ability to align the text left, right, or center. Some of them can even align justified such that the text is spread equally along the lines, so that the line endings of all lines are as near to the margins as possible.

Even though this kind of formatting is quite common in word processors, there are very few plain text editors that have this functionality, and Vim is one of them.

Vim supports three types of alignment—left aligned, right aligned, and centered. But before we look at how they work, we have to realize something about why this type of alignment is uncommon in plain text editors.

The fact is that in common text editors, there is no hidden information. The text you see is what you have—no page width, no alignments, nothing.

In word processors, on the other hand, there is a lot of information hidden in the document, and this tells the editor how to format text as the user wants it.

As this is not possible in text editors such as Vim, the user will have to supply the editor with information about the preferred text width—for example, in order to give the editor margins to align against.

With this in mind, let's take a look at the commands starting with how to center a text.

```
:[range]center WIDTH
```

Here, `range` is the range of lines you want to center, and `WIDTH` is the maximum number of characters you want on each line. Typically, you select the lines you want to center in the visual mode (use *Shift+v* and move the cursor to select lines) and then start typing in the command. You will see that after pressing :, Vim automatically adds the range you have selected as `'<, '>`. This basically means from first selected line (`'<`) to the last selected line (`'>`).

Next, you just have to write `center` and the width you want the text to have. You can leave out the width if you have set the Vim option, `textwidth`.

If the option is set to `0` and you still leave out the width, then Vim just expects you to want a text width of 80 characters. It probably won't take you long to realize that the text is not centered as in a word processor, but simply indented the correct amount with whitespaces. This also means that whenever you change the text in the centered line, you will have to re-center the text.

The next command is the left-align command:

`:[range]left INDENT`

Again, this command needs a range of lines to work on and, if needed, a number of characters to indent all the lines with. This means that you can set the left margin of those lines exactly where you want it.

Finally, there is the right-align command, which aligns the lines with the right margin. Again, there is the problem that Vim does not necessarily know the width of the text, and hence you have to supply it with this information. The command is as follows:

`:[range]right WIDTH`

The lines are again indented with whitespaces such that the line ends are all aligned according to the width you define. As with centered text, you will have to re-align the text whenever you change anything in a line because it will grow beyond the right margin.

Marking headlines

When you write documents in a plain text editor, you sometimes need to create your own formatting and markup in order to make the text more readable.

To improve readability, one of the major things that you can do is mark the strings that act as headlines for the sections of text.

In word processors, this is normally done by making the font larger and bold, but in Vim this is not possible because only one font size is allowed in the document. So, Vim users will have to mark the headlines another way.

My personal way of marking a line as a headline is by adding a line underneath it.

An example could be:

```
My Headline
===========
This is the text on the document. It could contain one
or more lines of text.
```

Different types of marks could be used for different levels of headlines:

```
Level1
======
Level2
------
-Level3-
```

To make it easier to add the underlining of the headlines, it can be wrapped in a macro in Vim. This way you don't have to worry whether you have added less / too much underlining of the headline.

A macro for the first two levels of headlines could look like this:

```
yypVr=o
```

Broken down in parts, this says:

- yy: Yank the current line
- p: Paste the copied line
- v: Select the entire line
- r: Replace the selected characters with the following characters (in this case, =)
- o: Add a new line below the cursor and place cursor on it in the insert mode

This macro basically takes the current line (the headline line) and duplicates it. Then it takes the duplicate and replaces all characters in it with some character (- or = in this case). Finally, it inserts a new line and goes back into the insert mode.

In the case of the third headline level, we have to take another approach as it is not an underlining, but rather an appending or a prepending of a dash (headline). For this, a simple substitution could be used.

```
:s/\(.*\)/-\1-/
```

If we again break it into pieces, it consists of three main parts:

- `:s///`: The substitution command.
- `\(.*\)`: Regular expression that takes all characters in the current line and remembers that this is the search pattern.
- `-\1-`: This is the replacement pattern. It tells Vim to insert a dash followed by the first matched subpattern (everything between `\(` and `\)`) from the previously mentioned search, followed by another dash.

Remembering these macros can be a bit hard, but you can easily create Vim mappings such that you can have a shortcut for each of the headline markings, for example:

```
:map h1 yypVr=o
```

```
:map h2 yypVr-o
```

```
:map h3 :s/\(.+\)/-\1-/<cr>o
```

Now, you can just go into the normal mode and press `h1`, `h2`, or `h3` to add the appropriate headline-level formatting. If you don't want it to insert an empty line under the headline and go into the insert mode, then simply remove the `o` from the end of each mapping.

Creating lists

Bullet lists and numbered lists are common structures in documents. In this recipe, we will look at how to make the task of creating these lists in Vim a lot easier.

Let's start by looking at how we can create a Vim function that takes a range of selected lines and converts them into a bullet list. In this case, a bullet list looks like this:

```
* first item
* second item
* third item
```

So, a function that adds `*` to the beginning of all the selected lines could look like this:

```
function! BulletList()
    let lineno = line(".")
    call setline(lineno, "    * " . getline(lineno))
endfunction
```

Looking at this quite simple function, you will see that all it does is get the current line and replace it with a copy of itself, prepended with a couple of spaces, a bullet (in this case an *), and then a tab space.

Obviously, it only does its work on one line. However, if you select a range of lines, Vim will call this function over and over again for each selected line – starting from the top down. This works fine when you need to add the same to every line and don't have to tell them apart.

However, this is not the case for numbered lists because you have to know how far in the numbers you have gotten.

So, let's take a look at a function that converts a range of selected lines into a numbered list – one line for each item:

```
function! NumberList() range
    " set line numbers in front of lines
    let beginning=line("'<")
    let ending= line("'>")
    let difsize = ending-beginning +1
    let pre = ' '
    while (beginning <= ending)
        if match(difsize, '^9*$') == 0
            let pre = pre . ' '
        endif
        call setline(ending, pre . difsize . "\t" . getline(ending))
        let ending=ending-1
        let difsize=difsize-1
    endwhile
endfunction
```

This function is a bit more complex; without losing the simplicity of the task it should solve – adding numbers in front of each selected line.

However this function does add a little extra to that – it right aligns the numbers like this:

```
  1 item1
  2 item2
 . . .
 10 item10
 11 item11
 . . .
100 item100
 . . .
```

In order to perform this alignment, it needs to take care of two issues:

- It needs to know the largest number in the list
- It needs to be able to work on all the lines at once

The first issue is handled by looking at the line number of the first and the last line in the selected range, and the difference is then the number of lines. Thus we get the largest number in the numbered list. This is only possible because the second issue is also taken care of, without which the function would only know about the current line.

The solution for this is simply to add the `range` keyword after the function name, and thereby tell Vim that the function will work on the entire range and not just one line.

The function goes through the lines in the range from the last line to the first. Whenever it hits a number that contains only the number 9 (such as 99 or 9999), it knows that it has one character less in the number (for example, going from line 1000 to line 999). Instead of the character it now misses, it simply prepends an extra space to the indentation. This way the numbers are kept right-aligned all the time, no matter how many lines you select to have in your range.

On `http://www.vimoutliner.org`, you can find a Vim script that uses headline formatting, list formatting, and so on to do outlining documents. If you like to do outlining in Vim, this is the script to use.

Formatting code

Formatting code often depends on many different things. Each programming language has its own syntax, and some languages rely on formatting like indentation more than others. In some cases, the programmer is following style guidelines given by an employer so that code can follow the company-wide style.

So, how should Vim know how you want your code to be formatted? The short answer is that it shouldn't! But by being flexible, Vim can let you set up exactly how you want your formatting done.

However, the fact is that even though formatting differs, most styles of formatting follow the same basic rules. This means that in reality, you only have to change the things that differ. In most cases, the changes can be handled by changing a range of settings in Vim. Among these, there are a few especially worth mentioning:

- `Formatoptions`: This setting holds formatting-specific settings (see `:help 'fo'`)
- `Comments`: What are comments and how they should be formatted (see `:help 'co'`)
- `(no)expandtab`: Convert tabs to spaces (see `:help 'expandtab'`)
- `Softtabstop`: How many spaces a single tab is converted to (see `:help 'sts'`)
- `Tabstop`: How many spaces a tab looks like (see `:help 'ts'`)

With these options, you can set nearly every aspect of how Vim will indent your code, and whether it should use spaces or tabs for indentation. But this is not enough because you still have to tell Vim if it should actually try to do the indentation for you, or if you want to do it manually. If you want Vim to do the indentation for you, you have the choice between four different ways for Vim to do it. In the following sections, we will look at the options you can set to interact with the way Vim indents code.

Autoindent

Autoindent is the simplest way of getting Vim to indent your code. It simply stays at the same indentation level as the previous line. So, if the current line is indented with four spaces, then the new line you add by pressing *Enter* will automatically be indented with four spaces too. It is then up to you as to how and when the indentation level needs to change again. This type of indentation is particularly good for languages where the indentation stays the same for several lines in a row. You get autoindent by using `:set, autoindent,` or `:set ai`.

Smartindent

Smartindent is the next step when you want a smarter indent than autoindent. It still gives you the indentation from the previous line, but you don't have to change the indentation level yourself. Smartindent recognizes the most common structures from the C programming language and uses this as a marker for when to add / remove the indentation levels. As many languages are loosely based on the same syntax as C, this will work for those languages as well. You get smart indent by using any of the following commands:

- `:set smartindent`
- `:set si.`

Cindent

Cindent is often called clever indent or configurable indent because it is more configurable than the previous two indentation methods. You have access to three different setup options:

`cinkeys`	This option contains a comma-separated list of keys that Vim should use to change the indentation level. An example could be: `:set cinkeys="0{,0},0#,:"`, which means that it should reindent whenever it hits a {, a } or a # as the first character on the line, or if you use : as the last character on the line (as used in switch constructs in many languages). The default value for cinkeys is `"0{, 0}, 0), :, 0#, !^F, o, O,` and e". See `:help cinkeys` for more information on what else you can set in this option.
`cinoptions`	This option contains all the special options you can set specifically for cindent. A large range of options can be set in this comma-separated list. An example could be: `:set cinoptions=">2,{3,}3"`, which means that we want Vim to add two extra spaces to the normal indent length, and we want to place { and } three spaces as compared to the previous line. So, if we have a normal indent to be four spaces, then the previous example could result in the code looking like this (dot marks represent a space):

```
if( a == b)
...{
......print "hello";
...}
```

The default value for cinoptions is this quite long string: `">s,e0, n0,f0,{0,}0,^0,:s,=s,l0,b0,gs,hs,ps,ts,is,+s,c3,C0,/0,( 2s,us,U0,w0,W0,m0,j0,)20,*30"`. See `:help 'cinoptions'` for more information on all the options.

`cinwords`	This option contains all the special keywords that will make Vim add indentation on the next line. An example could be: `:set cinwords="if,else,do,while,for,switch"`, which is also the default value for this option. See `:help 'cinwords'` for more information.

Indentexpr

Indentexpr is the most flexible indent option to use, but also the most complex. When used, indentexpr evaluates an expression to compute the indent of a line. Hence, you have to write an expression that Vim can evaluate. You can activate this option by simply setting it to a specific expression such as:

```
:set indentexpr=MyIndenter()
```

Here, `MyIndenter()` is a function that computes the indentation for the lines it is executed on.

A very simple example could be a function that emulates the autoindent option:

```
function! MyIndenter()
   " Find previous line and get its indentation
   let prev_lineno = s:prevnonblank(v:lnum)
   let ind = indent( prev_lineno )
   return ind
endfunction
```

Adding just a bit more functionality than this, the complexity increases quite fast. Vim comes with a lot of different indent expressions for many programming languages. These can serve as inspiration if you want to write your own indent expression. You can find them in the `indent` folder in your VIMHOME.

You can read more about how to use indentexpr in `:help 'indentexpr'` and `:help 'indent-expression'`.

Fast code-block formatting

After you have configured your code formatting, you might want to update your code to follow these settings. To do so, you simply have to tell Vim that it should reindent every single line in the file from the first line to the last. This can be done with the following Vim command:

```
1G=G
```

If we split it up, it simply says:

1G: Go to the first line of the file (alternatively you can use gg)

=: Equalize lines; in other words, indent according to formatting configuration

G: Go to the last line in the file (tells Vim where to end indenting)

You could easily map this command to a key in order to make it easily accessible:

```
:nmap <F11> 1G=G
```

```
:imap <F11> <ESC>1G=Ga
```

The last a is to get back into the insert mode as this was where we originally were. So, now you can just press the *F11* key in order to reindent the entire buffer correctly.

> Note that if you have a programmatic error, for example, missing a semicolon at the end of a line in a C program, the file will not be correctly indented from that point on in the buffer. This can sometimes be useful to identify where a scope is not closed correctly (for example, a { not closed with a }).

Sometimes, you might just want to format smaller blocks of code. In those cases, you typically have two options—use the natural scope blocks in the code, or select a block of code in the visual mode and indent it.

The last one is simple. Go into the visual mode with, for example, *Shift+v* and then press = to reindent the lines.

When it comes to using code blocks on the other hand, there are several different ways to do it. In Vim, there are multiple ways to select a block of code. So in order to combine a command that indents a code block, we need to look at the different types and the commands to select them:

i{	**Inner block**, which means everything between { and } excluding the brackets. This can also be selected with i} and iB.
a{	**A block**, which means all the code between { and } including the brackets. This can also be selected with a} and aB.
i(	**Inner parenthesis**, meaning everything between (and) excluding the parentheses. Can also be selected with i) and ib.
a(	**A parentheses**, meaning everything between (and) including the parenthesis. Can also be selected with a) and ab.
i<	**Inner < > block**, meaning everything between < and > excluding the brackets. Can also be selected with i>.
a<	**A < > block**, meaning everything between < and > including the brackets. Can also be selected with a>.
i[	**Inner [ ] block**, meaning everything between [and] excluding the square brackets. Can also be selected with i].
a[	**A [ ] block**, meaning everything between [and], including the square brackets. This can also be selected with a].

So, we have defined what Vim sees a block of code as; now, we simply have to tell it what to do with the block. In our case, we want to reindent the code. We already know that = can do this. So, an example of a code block reindentation could look like this:

```
=i{
```

Let's execute the code block reindentation in the following code (| being the place where the cursor is):

```
if( a == b )
   {
     print |"a equals b";
   }
```

This would produce the following code (with default C format settings):

```
if( a == b )
   {
     print |"a equals b";
   }
```

If, on the other hand, we choose to use a{ as the block we are working on, then the resulting code would look like this:

```
if( a == b )
   {
     print "a equals b";
   }
```

As you can see in the last piece of code, the =a{ command corrects the indentation of both the brackets and the print line.

In some cases where you work in a code block with multiple levels of code blocks, you might want to reindent the current block and maybe the surrounding one. No worries, Vim has a fast way to do this. If, for instance, you want to reindent the current code block and besides that want to reindent the block that surrounds it, you simply have to execute the following command while the cursor is placed in the innermost block:

```
=2i{
```

This simply tells Vim that you will equalize / reindent two levels of inner blocks counting from the "active" block and out. You can replace the number 2 with any number of levels of code blocks you want to reindent. Of course, you can also swap the inner block command with any of the other block commands, and that way select exactly what you want to reindent.

So, this is really all it takes to get your code to indent according to the setup you have.

Auto format pasted code

The trend among programmers tells us that we tend to reuse parts of our code, or so-called patterns. This could mean that you have to do a lot of copying and pasting of code.

Most users of Vim have experienced what is often referred to as the **stair effect** when pasting code into a file. This effect occurs when Vim tries to indent the code as it inserts it. This often results in each new line to be indented to another level, and you ending up with a stair:

```
code line 1
   code line 2
      codeline 3
         code line 4
      . . .
```

The normal workaround for this is to go into the `paste`-mode in Vim, which is done by using:

`:set paste`

After pasting your code, you can now go back to your normal insert mode again:

`:set nopaste`

But what if there was another workaround? What if Vim could automatically indent the pasted code such that it is indented according to the rest of the code in the file? Vim can do that for you with a simple paste command.

`p=`]`

This command simply combines the normal paste command (p) with a command that indents the previously inserted lines (=`]). It actually relies on the fact that when you paste with p (lowercase), the cursor stays on the first character of the pasted text. This is combined with `], which takes you to the last character of the latest inserted text and gives you a motion across the pasted text from the first line to the last.

So, all you have to do now is map this command to a key and then use this key whenever you paste a piece of code into your file.

Using external formatting tools

Even though experienced Vim users often say that Vim can do everything, this is of course not the truth—but is close. For those things that Vim can't do, it is smart enough to be able to use external tools.

In the following sections, we will take a look at some of the most used external tools that can be used for formatting your code, and how to use them.

Indent

The Indent program is probably one of the most used external programs for Vim. It has been around since the late 80s for various Unix platforms, and has also later been imported to other platforms including Microsoft Windows.

As the name indicates, this program indents code—especially the code that resembles the C code in syntax. What you may wonder is why you would use an external program for this when Vim can handle this task just fine. This is a good question because Vim can do this very well, but the Indent program does it better and at the same time makes it easier to standardize the indentation among multiple editors.

By specializing only in indenting code, indent is able to indent code more effectively than the limited indent functionality included in Vim, for which indenting is "a feature" and not "the feature". Indent specializes in understanding the code and indents it according to the code—even if there is a syntactic error in the code.

So, how do you use Indent from within Vim? Previously, we have seen several different options for how Vim should indent your code. There is, however, one option that overrules all of them:

```
:set equalprog=PROGRAM
```

What this option does is set the external program that Vim should use for indentation when using the commands with = . In the case of Indent, you simply change PROGRAM to the path to your Indent program. Now, whenever you use one of the indentation commands such as 1G=G, it takes the involved lines and pipes them through the program you have defined in equalprog. You can even supply the program with command-line arguments if needed.

In the case of Indent, there are so many different command-line arguments that you will get a better result by configuring its configuration file.

You can always find the latest version of the Indent program at this address: http://www.gnu.org/software/indent/.

Berkeley Par

In the early 90s, Adam M. Costello began working on a simple command-line program whose only purpose was to reformat a given text with a paragraph in it according to the user's wishes. The program was called Par and, within a year or two, it evolved into a very feature-rich program that could reformat nearly any type of paragraph.

This, of course, makes Par an ideal external friend for Vim. So, let's look at some examples of how it can be used.

If, for instance, you want your text to be nicely formatted in paragraphs with no more than 78 characters on each line, then you could simply use it as:

```
:set formatprg=par\ -w78
```

The `formatprg` option in Vim tells it which program to use for formatting of the text when one of the `gq` commands is used. Notice that the space between the program name and its option is escaped with a backslash. This is needed in order for Vim to see the entire string as one option and not two.

 Note that Vim will only use `formatprg` when `formatexpr` is empty. Otherwise, the `formatexpr` will be used.

From earlier on, we know that Vim cannot justify the text such that both ends of the lines are aligned with the margins. Fortunately, Par can help us here. By simply adding a `j` (for "justify") to our previous `formatprg` value, we can get Par to justify the text:

```
:set formatprg=par\ -w78j
```

Par cannot only be used on a normal text, but also on some parts of the code—the comments.

If you, for instance, have the following comment:

```
/*********************************************************************/
/* This function helps you modify a string and remove all */
/* unnecessary  characters .  */
/* Don't use this on widechar strings or strings shorter than 10 */
/* characters */
/*********************************************************************/
```

You could select it in Vim and then do:

```
!par 60r
```

(Vim adds `'<, '>` in front of `!` as a range).

This will give you the following result:

```
/*********************************************************/
/* This function helps you modify a string and remove all */
/* unnecessary characters . Don't use this on widechar    */
/* strings or strings shorter than 10 characters          */
/*********************************************************/
```

With a single command, you have transformed an ugly, unformatted comment into a nicely formatted and aligned comment.

The manual page for Par gives a lot of examples on what else it is capable of.

> You could easily map different Par commands to different keys in Vim and this way have formatting keys for all text, comments, lists, and so on.

Tidy

If you work with web development or XML files, the tidy program could easily become your next best friend besides Vim. This program cleans up the code that is fed to it and makes it compliant for the **World Wide Web Consortium (W3C)** . Being W3C-compliant means that the code is constructed such that it follows the HTML guidelines set by the (W3C).

As a web programmer, I once in a while get in a situation where I have to open someone else's HTML or XML file only to find that it is one big mess. Because of this, I run all files with the `.xml`, `.htm`, or `.html` extension through tidy when opening it. This is done using autocommands (au for short) in Vim, which I have added to my vimrc file.

For XML this looks as follows:

```
au FileType xml exe ":silent 1,$!tidy --input-xml true --indent yes
-q"
```

For HTML files, it looks like this:

```
au FileType html,htm exe ":silent 1,$!tidy --indent yes -q"
```

Please note that this will alter the file you open without you knowing anything about what it has changed. In both cases, Vim expects to find a program called tidy in your path, no matter if you are in Linux or Windows.

As you can see from the arguments I have given for the tidy program, it can also be used for reformatting the indentation of the HTML / XML. This option makes the file very readable and it gets a lot easier to get an overview of a file after opening it.

Since tidy checks for errors in the document, you could assign it to a key, so that at any time you could check if the changes you have made are in fact W3C compliant.

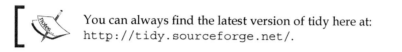

You can always find the latest version of tidy here at: http://tidy.sourceforge.net/.

Summary

In this chapter, we have looked at how to get better at formatting both our text and code.

First, we looked at how you can format your text into easily readable paragraphs with the help of a couple of simple Vim commands. We also looked at how to justify the text and why this is not normally so easy to achieve in a plain text editor such as Vim. Next, we created functions for marking headlines and generating both bulleted lists and numbered lists. We learned that Vim is very flexible and you can tell it, for instance, whether you want to get it to run your function once for each line you have selected, or whether it should simply let you handle it and feed your function with all the lines at once.

From here we moved on to looking at how to format your code in Vim, and especially how to indent code. We learned that since we all have our own special coding style, it is often hard to make a generic functionality for code formatting. Vim handles this by giving the user a flexible interface for setting up exactly how he or she wants it to format the code. We also looked at a couple of recipes for how we can format a block of code fast, and even how to format the code that you paste into Vim from other places.

Finally, we took a look at how we can use an external tool to give Vim that extra edge it needs to be the perfect editor. External tools can help you format both text and code, and we took a short look at some of the most popular ones to see how they can work together with Vim.

At this point, you should be pretty comfortable with modifying Vim to your needs by using the built-in functions. Now, let's move on to the next chapter and look at how you can extend Vim by writing your own Vim scripts.

6
Basic Vim Scripting

One of Vim's most powerful features is the extensibility it offers by allowing power users to write scripts. With this feature, you can add nearly any feature to Vim and easily share it with other Vim users.

In this chapter, we will look at some of the basic aspects of script writing for Vim. The chapter will contain recipes focusing on the following subjects:

- Creating syntax-coloring scripts for Vim
- How to install and use scripts in Vim
- Different types of scripts
- How to develop scripts in Vim
- Basic syntax of a Vim script
- How to use other scripting languages when writing Vim scripts

After you have read this chapter, you should have a basic idea about how to use the script functionality in Vim. You should also be able to write your own simple scripts for Vim and, thereby, be able to add features to Vim.

Syntax-color schemes

For many programmers, the ability to get the code colored according to the syntax is one of the most important features in Vim. Syntax coloring gives both a better overview of the code and can help the user discover errors in the code. In Vim, the syntax-coloring system uses script files that very much resemble a Vim script file — they just define colors rather than functionality. In the following section, we will take a look at how to create such a syntax-color scheme.

Your first syntax-color file

Looking at syntax coloring in a simple way, it's all about identifying certain words and structures in the text, and then giving them the correct color according to what they are. In most cases, however, it is a bit more advanced than that. The syntax-coloring needs to be context-aware in order to be usable. Let's look at an example where we have the following code that we want to syntax color:

```
/* if x equals y then return the value */
if (x == y)
  {
    return x;
  }
```

If we simply match on words and symbols, we could get quite a good result. This is done with the following match strings in Vim (as previously described in Chapter 2, *Personalizing Vim*):

```
:syntax keyword myVars x y
:syntax match mySymbols "[{}();=]"
:syntax keyword myKeywords if return
:highlight myVars ctermfg=red guifg=red
:highlight mySymbols ctermfg=blue guifg=blue
:highlight myKeywords ctermfg=green guifg=green
```

The result is shown in the following screenshot:

As you can see, the code part is acceptably syntax-colored, but what about the comment part of the code? Because we just match on single words, the same words in the comment are matched too, and hence get the same color as the code. This makes it very hard to distinguish the comments from the code.

So, what have we learned from this little example? There is, in fact, more to syntax coloring than finding words and giving them colors. So, let's add a bit of context awareness by saying that it should look for anything between /* and */, and mark it as a comment, and then go on and syntax color the rest. The parts of the code that have been colored once will not be colored again by other rules. Hence, the order of the rules matter. The code for doing this in Vim could look like:

```
:syntax match myComments "/\*.*\*/"
:syntax keyword myVars x y
:syntax match mySymbols "[{}();=]"
:syntax keyword myKeywords if return
:highlight myVars ctermfg=red guifg=red
:highlight mySymbols ctermfg=blue guifg=blue
:highlight myKeywords ctermfg=green guifg=green
:highlight myComments ctermfg=yellow guifg=yellow
```

This results in the code looking like this:

So, now we actually have a decent syntax coloring for this little piece of code. Of course, this is just a small example and it uses a very limited amount of the syntax-coloring functionality in Vim. Let's move on and take a look at some of the other possibilities you have.

Syntax regions

In our previous example, we selected the comment line using the `match` option for the syntax command. In some cases, however, it is hard to create a suitable match and other simpler approaches are needed.

In Vim, you can select entire regions of the code and color them, simply by setting what a region starts with and what it ends with. To build on our previous example, let's make a region-syntax command to substitute our old match command:

```
:syntax region myComments start=/\/\*/ end=/\*\//
```

With this command, I can easily match any of the following comment blocks:

```
/* single line comment */
/**********************************
 *   multi line comments
 *********************************/
/* multi line comment
 */
```

But the `region` option can do more than just setting what a region starts and ends with. It also allows you to set which other things inside the region you want to be colored by other syntax rules. One thing I often use is the ability to give keywords in my function comments such as FIXME, OBSOLETE, TODO, and so on, so that I could have the code like this:

```
/*   function: splitString()
 *   args    : string
 *   OBSOLETE
 */
function splitString(string){
 . . .
```

All we have to do now is make a keyword group that colors the specific keyword like this:

`:syntax keyword myKeywords OBSOLETE FIXME TODO`

We have to modify the region command in order to tell that it is allowed to contain other syntax elements. The command will then look like this:

`:syntax region myComments start=/\/\*/ end=/\*\// contains=myKeywords`

If more than one syntax group needs to be containable inside your region, then you simply add them in the `contains` list separated by a comma.

> You can tell Vim that a region is correct only if both the start and end are on the same line, by adding the one-line option to your syntax command. Without this option, Vim will start syntax coloring the code from when it hits the start, until it hits the matching end (or the end of the file).

At some point, you might want a region to be able to be nested inside another region. In that case, you will have to tell Vim that it should make this possible. You do so by adding the `contained` option to the end of your region command:

```
:syntax region myComments start=/\/\*/ end=/\*\// contains=myKeywords
contained
```

In some cases, a block could be anything else in the code, and then of course you don't want to write all the syntax groups. Here, you simply set `contains` to be `ALL`.

Other keywords such as `ALL` exist in Vim:

ALLBUT	If this is the first item in the list, then all subsequent syntax groups in the list will not be able to be colored in this region
CONTAINED	If this is in the list, then the syntax groups with the `contained` option are able to be syntax-colored in this region
TOP	If this is in the list, then all the syntax groups except those having the `contained` option are included

With these you can easily select a large range of syntax groups without having to write them all down. An example could be to select all but the `myComments` group. This is done with the following:

```
:syntax region myCodeblock start=/{/ end=/}/ contains=ALLBUT,myComments
```

> If you know that some syntax groups are often used together, then you can join them into a cluster: `:syntax cluster myCluster contains=myKeywords,mySymbols,myConditions`. A cluster can be used by adding a @ in front of the name: `:syntax region myComments start=/\/\*/ end=/\*\// contains=@myCluster`.

Now, all you have to do is combine everything in one file and place it in a directory called `syntax` in your VIMHOME. The name of the file needs to be the name of the file type you use for your programming language files appended with `.vim`. This means that example files with the C programming language have the `.c` file extension and hence their syntax file is called `c.vim`.

In the previous examples, all my syntax group names are prepended with `my`, which is because the syntax for my programming language is called `my` (imaginary, of course). Had it been the syntax for the C programming language instead, then it would be a good idea to give all the groups names that begin with c (`cKeywords`, `cConditions`, `cSymbols`, and so on.).

Just to follow the example, we say that the files in the programming language are named with a `.my` file extension. For simplicity, I want Vim to know my files as having the `my` file type.

If the file type you are using for your files is not known by Vim, then you have to register it for the syntax file to work. This is done by adding a couple of lines to your `filetype.vim` file in your VIMHOME. If the file does not exist, then simply create it. In the case of the My programming language, I would need to add the following lines:

```
augroup filetypedetect
autocmd BufNewFile,BufRead *.my      setfiletype my
augroup END
```

This code tells Vim that it should add everything between the two `augroup` lines to the `filetypedetect` auto-command group. This is the group of commands that Vim uses to figure out which file type to give a file that it opens or works on.

In our case, it simply adds a line that makes Vim set the file type to my whenever it creates or opens a file with the `.my` extension. Many other `autocmd` lines could be added in between the `augroup` lines if you need it to distinguish from other file types as well.

Now that Vim detects we are working on files with the my file type, it automatically looks for a matching syntax file. It does this by looking in your VIMHOME/syntax/ directory for a file with a name matching the file type—in this case, my.vim.

This is all you need to get started on creating your own syntax files that Vim can automatically load whenever you open one of your files.

> The best way to learn about how to create a syntax file is by looking at other people's syntax files. Vim comes bundled with syntax files for a wide variety of file types you can use as inspiration or extend with your own commands.

On the other hand, if you just want to add some extra syntax recognition to an already existing syntax file, you have two options. You could, of course, find the existing syntax file on your system and modify it with your additions. A better solution, however, would be to use the post-processing feature in Vim, which makes it possible to overwrite existing scripting, syntax, and so on that Vim has already loaded. This way, whenever a script is updated on your system, you don't have to add your changes again because they are completely separated from the script itself.

The secret of how to use the post processor is all about where you place your script files. In your VIMHOME, you have a directory called `after` (if it does not exist, simply create it). Whenever Vim looks for a script, syntax file, or color scheme in your runtime path and finds it, it looks for the same file in the `after` directory. So, if it found the VIMHOME/syntax/c.vim file, then it looks for a file named VIMHOME/after/syntax/c.vim to see if there is anything from the first file it should overwrite. The same is the case for scripts found in any of the following directories:

- plugin
- ftplugin
- indent
- autoload
- syntax
- colors

You just add any of these directories to your `after` directory whenever you need a file to be placed in it. If Vim finds it, it will use it.

Color scheme and syntax coloring

In our previous example, we added our own highlighting color groups with the `:syntax` command in Vim. This gives you complete control over the colors, but you also limit yourself to use only those colors. Hence, it might not follow the colors defined by the color scheme you use in the rest of Vim.

A better approach is to use the color groups already defined in Vim, and thereby split the color definition and syntax highlighting into two parts. This way, whenever you change the color scheme in Vim, your syntax coloring will change accordingly.

You can find a list of all defined colors by using this command:

`:highlight`

 Or, you can take a look inside one of the color scheme files available for Vim. You will find the color schemes in a folder called `color` in your VIMHOME, or wherever your Vim has been installed.

Using scripts

We all have some particular features that we simply can't live without in our editor of choice. Some features are simple modifications such as specific key bindings, while others are large and complex extensions throughout the entire editor. Of course, Vim will not be able to satisfy everyone's needs, so instead it opens up for developers to extend through scripts.

What if you are not a programmer, or do not have the time to develop your own scripts for Vim? Not a problem. Vim is given away free of charge under the charity license; a lot of script developers have decided that they will also give away the scripts they have developed for free. Many of them even put their scripts for easy download on the online Vim community site `http://www.vim.org`, which means that you can easily search for scripts that do exactly what you want them to do.

Script types

On the Vim Community site, you will find scripts that solve many kinds of tasks, ranging from simple things such as inserting the date in the text to full programming IDEs inside Vim. But actually, there are some defined groups of script types that Vim knows of.

If we look at the script types that add features to Vim, we can split them into two groups. The first group is the **Global** plugins group, which consists of scripts that will be initialized when Vim starts or when the user executes some specific function call. This kind of script is typically used for adding menus to Gvim, adding extra functionality to already existing functions in Vim, or maybe changing some feature in Vim to fit the user's need.

The second group is the **File-Type** plugins group. Scripts in this group are bound to a particular file type (or multiple file types), and the script is only loaded whenever a file of this type is opened or created. The functionality of the scripts in this group could be adding features specific to a particular file type, or the tools used in relation to it. An example could be adding key bindings that make it easy to call a compiler for a certain programming language, or it could be a function that automatically adds a comment above all functions a programmer writes. The scripts in this group also include the scripts for adding syntax coloring, though these are often installed elsewhere than the rest of the scripts in this group.

Installing scripts

When you download scripts, they typically come in one of the three formats:

- As a single `.vim` script file
- As a compressed (typically Zip) file that typically contains one or more `.vim` files (both global and file type-dependent) and documentation.
- As a Vimball, which is an automatic Vim script installation written in Vim

If the script you want to install is just a Vim script file, then normally all it takes to install it is to copy it to the `VIMHOME/plugin` directory, or `VIMHOME/ftplugin` if it is a file type-dependent script.

If you are on a multiuser system, you can install it for all users at the same time by installing it in directories with the same names, instead of in your VIMHOME, which is located where Vim is installed on your system.

If the script comes in a compressed file instead, it can be hard to tell how to install it. Typically, you will simply have to place the file in your VIMHOME and then uncompress it there. This normally places the files in the right folders according to how Vim wants them. In any case, there might be a README or INSTALL file where you can read how to install the script.

If you have found the script on the online Vim Community at http://www.vim.org, then you will find instructions for installation on the page that describes the script.

The third and last way to install Vim scripts is by using the Vimball installation system—an installation system created for Vim 7 and newer. This system takes a range of files and combines them into a single Vim script archive with the extension .vba—a Vimball.

Before you start using Vimballs, you will need to have the Vimball script installed. This adds the functionality for reading and installing Vimballs. As with most other scripts for Vim, you will be able to find the script on the online Vim community site.

The latest version of the Vimball script can always be found here at: http://www.vim.org/scripts/script.php?script_id=1502.

When you have the Vimball script installed, you are ready to use Vimballs for installing other Vim scripts.

Let's say that you have a Vimball called myscript.vba and want to install it. You simply open the Vimball in Vim. Vim will now tell you how to install the script. This is normally done by executing the following command:

```
:source %
```

This installs the script in the first place found in the runtimepath option in Vim. If you want to install the script elsewhere, you can do so by using the following command instead:

```
:UseVimball PATH
```

You need to replace PATH with the path where you want Vim to install the script. Please note that some scripts only work when they are installed in the correct place.

Sometimes, you do not want to install a script unless you know what it contains. If this is the case, then the Vimball script has a command that will give you a list of the files that you will get installed if you decide to install the Vimball. To get the list of files in the Vimball, execute the following command after you have opened the Vimball in Vim:

`:VimballList`

If the files and directories listed are the ones you expected, then you are ready to install the file, and can then use either the `:source` or the `:UseVimball` command to install it.

Uninstalling scripts

There is normally no automatic way of uninstalling scripts after they are installed, and you will have to go through the files one by one and uninstall them manually. Having said that, the Vimball script does, in fact, have an uninstall mechanism.

If you remember the name of the Vimball you used to install a Vim script, then you can later use this very same Vimball name to uninstall the script. You just have to execute the following command in Vim:

`:RmVimball VIMBALLNAME`

Replace the VIMBALLNAME with the name of the Vimball you used to install the script. If the script was not installed in the default place (if installed with `:UseVimball`), then you can add the installation path as a second argument to the command, and thereby tell the Vimball script where to find the files it should remove.

`:RmVimball VIMBALLNAME PATH`

In order to be able to bind a Vimball name to the files it needs to delete, the script will create a file called `.VimballRecord` in your VIMHOME. Note that if you remove this file, you will not be able to uninstall any of the Vimballs you have previously installed unless you do it manually.

Script development

At some point when using Vim, you might find a feature it does not have, and which you need it to have. So now is probably a good time to learn how to make your own scripts for Vim such that you can add this missing functionality.

However, before you start, there are a couple of questions you should consider.

First of all, you should make sure that no one else has already created a script that adds what you need — why invent the wheel again? If someone has created a script that does nearly what you need, then why not just help the developer by adding the extra features to that script and thereby make it work for both him or her and you? This shortens the development time and limits the number of similar scripts floating around.

If you didn't find any scripts that matched your needs, you need to get working on the script. In this case, you should consider from the start whether or not you want to distribute your script to others when it is done. Bram Moolenaar released Vim free of charge for you to use, and other Vim script developers have done the same with their scripts. I would urge you to get into the spirit of sharing and do the same with your Vim scripts.

> You can find out more about open source licenses on this address: http://www.opensource.org/.

In case you do decide to share your scripts, you should (from the beginning) remember that Vim is available for a wide variety of platforms and it would be preferable for your script to work on those too. This basically means that:

- You should never expect that some external program is available
- You should never expect that an external program is installed where you have it installed
- You should remember that file systems are different on different platforms
- You should remember that some Vim functionalities are available only on some platforms
- You should try to make things as configurable as possible — others might not want things how you want them

With this in mind, you are ready to start looking at how Vim scripts are put together. So, let's move on to look at some actual Vim script code.

Script writing basics

In the next few sections, we will take a look at all the basic types and structures you will need to know in order to be able to write a good Vim script.

If you are already a programmer who knows one or more programming languages, or scripting languages, then you will most likely find many similarities between them and how the Vim scripting language is constructed.

Types

In Vim there are, roughly speaking, only two types—strings and numbers. When I say roughly speaking, it is because within those two types there are other subtypes. A number can be represented in three different ways depending on how you want it:

- Decimal number: 1, 2, 3, 10, 100, and so on
- Hexadecimal: 0x01, 0x02, 0x03, 0x0A, 0x64
- Octal: 01, 02, 03, 012, 0144

Decimal numbers are used as they are, but you need to prepend hexadecimal numbers with 0x, and octal with 0. Vim will easily be able to use the numbers in calculations together, no matter if they are of the same kind or not. This means that you could easily make calculations saying:

```
:echo 10 + 0x0A + 012
```

This would result in Vim replying with 30.

In Vim, a string is represented as a normal text string encapsulated in either single quotes or double quotes, for example:

```
:echo "this is a string"
:echo 'this is a string'
```

If you need to use the character you used to encapsulate the string inside the string, then you can escape it with a backslash:

```
:echo "this is a string with a \" double quote"
:echo 'the double quote " does not need escaping here'
```

Whether to use single or double quotes depends on the situation.

In a single-quoted string, everything is shown as it is represented in the written string—also known as a literal string. This means that you cannot use special escaped characters in the string.

For example, this will work:

```
:echo "string with\n two lines"
```

But this won't:

```
:echo 'string with\n two lines'
```

Besides the newline character \n, there are others available in Vim:

\n	Newline, line break
\r	Carriage return
\t	Tab space
\123	Octal numbers (123 can be any number)
\x123	Hexadecimal number (123 can be any number)
\u	Character encoded as up to 4 hex numbers (for example, \u01fc34)
\f	Form feed
\e	Esc
\b	Backspace

Besides these escape characters, you can always insert the Vim-specific key acronyms such as <CR> and <ESC> by prepending them with a backslash—\<CR>. Even the Vim-specific key shortcuts (such as <C-W> for *Ctrl+W*) can be inserted by escaping them with a backslash.

Variables

In Vim, there are five types of variables, which (even though are defined the same way) can be used very differently. The five types are as follows:

- String: A simple string such as "this is a string"
- Number: A numeric value such as 123 or 0x123
- List: An ordered sequence of items (an ordered array)
- Dictionary: An unordered associative array holding key-value pairs
- Funcref: A reference to a function

The name of the variable can include alphanumeric characters and underscore. It cannot, however, start with a number and hence must start with a letter or an underscore.

Always use meaningful variable names if possible—remember that others might need to read and understand your code afterwards. To prevent your variables from conflicting with others' variables, you can make your variable names unique by—for example—prepending them with your initials like this: KSmyvariable. If there is more than one developer on the script, then you can instead use an abbreviation of the script name. For example, Vim sort script could have variables such as VSmyvariable or VSSmyvariable.

All of the variable types are defined with the `:let` command as follows:

```
:let myvar = VALUE
```

Here, VALUE depends on the type of the variable. In the case of strings and numbers, the value is simply defined as the types in Vim, for example:

```
:let mystringvar = "a string"
```

```
:let mynumbervar = 123
```

When working with string and number variables in Vim, there is an automatic conversion going on between the two types depending on how you use them. This means that even though you execute this:

```
:let mystringvar="123"
```

you can still use this:

```
:let mynumbervar=mystringvar-23
```

and `mystringvar` is automatically converted in place when the other number is subtracted from it.

 You can force a string to become a number by adding 0 to it, for example, `:let mynumber=mystringvar+0`. To force conversion from a number to a string, you can use the `string()` function: `:let mystring=string(mynumber)`.

This automatic conversion, however, stops when we move to lists and dictionaries because these can contain different types within their value. In the following table, you can see examples of how the automatic conversion works:

Input (type)	Result (type)
`"hello" . "world"` (string.string)	`"hello world"` (string)
`"number" . 123`	`"number 123"` (string)
`"123" + 10`	`133` (number)
`"123" - 10 . "hits"`	`"113 hits"` (string)
`"123" - 10 + "hits"`	`113` (number)

To define a list, use square brackets to enclose a comma-separated list of values:

```
:let mylistvar1 = [1,2,"three",0x04, myfivevar]
```

A list can contain other lists and hence can be a list of lists:

```
:let mylistvar2 = [[1,2,3],["four","five","six"]]
```

As you can see, the previous examples contain strings, numbers, and lists as item types in the list. This makes this type of variable very suitable as a storage container for various values.

Later, we will look at how to use the values in a list variable and how to work with multiple lists together.

If you want to create a variable of the type dictionary, it is done with the following `let` command:

```
:let mydictvar1 = {1: "one", 2: "two", 3: "three"}
```

This creates a dictionary with three items where the key is the number and the value is the number spelled out with letters (for example, 1 is the key and `"one"` is the value).

It does not matter whether you write a number key (as mentioned previously) or a string, as Vim will always convert it into a string. So, the previous example will actually define key-value pairs as `1:one`.

You can also create dictionaries with nested dictionaries. This is done as follows:

```
:let mydictvar2 =  {1: "one",2: "two","tens":{0: "ten",1: "eleven"}}
```

As you can see, the key doesn't have to follow any strict order, and doesn't have to be a number (see `"tens"` in the example).

Later, we will look at how to access the values in a dictionary, and how to move from dictionary to list and back.

The final variable type is the `funcref` type. This type can contain a reference to a function and can, in contrast to the other types, be executed. To define a `funcref` variable, use the following command:

```
:let Myfuncrefvar = function("Myfunction")
```

This ties the `Myfunction` function to the `Myfuncrefvar` variable. Notice that the variable name starts with a capital letter. This is because all user-defined function names in Vim need to have a capital first letter in the name, and hence all variables that can be executed as functions should have the same restriction.

To use a `funcref` variable later on, you simply use it as a normal variable name, except that you add parentheses after the name like this:

```
:echo Myfuncrefvar()
```

Alternatively, it can simply be called with the `:call` command:

```
:call Myfuncrefvar()
```

If the function tied to the variable takes arguments, then these are simply added in the parentheses like this: `Myfuncrefvar(arg1, arg2,...,argN)`.

When you work with variables in Vim, there are different scopes you can make them available in. This means that you can have some variables available only in a function, while others are global in Vim.

As a Vim script developer, you have to mark the variable yourself to tell Vim in which scope the variable should be available. This is done by adding a scope marker at the beginning of the variable name.

If you define a variable in Vim without specifying which scope it belongs to, then it belongs to the global scope by default—unless it is defined in a function, which causes it to only be available in the function itself. The following eight scopes are available:

- `v`: Vim predefined global scope
- `g`: Global scope
- `b`: Buffer scope—only available in the buffer where it was defined
- `t`: Tab scope—only available in the Vim tab where it was defined
- `w`: Window scope—only available to the current Vim window (viewport)
- `l`: Function scope—local to the function it is defined in
- `s`: Sourced file scope—local to a Vim script loaded using `:source`
- `a`: Argument scope—used in arguments for functions

 Did you know that comments in Vim scripts are created by having a quote as the first non-space character on the line: `" this is a comment?`

So for an example that uses some of the scope names, we could look at the following function:

```
let g:sum=0
function SumNumbers(num1,num2)
    let l:sum = a:num1+a:num2
    "check if previous sum was lower than this
    if g:sum < l:sum
        let g:sum=l:sum
    endif
    return l:sum
endfunction
" test code, this will print 7 (value of l:sum)
```

```
echo SumNumbers(3,4)
" this should also print  7 (value of g:sum)
echo g:sum
```

Even though you are able to have both local and global variables with the same naming, it is in general a bad practice to use the same names in a local scope if you already know that it is in use in the global scope.

 Try to use the correct scopes whenever possible. This way you can prevent the global scope from overflowing with variables you do not control and whose origin you do not know.

Conditions

When creating a script for Vim, it is often necessary to be able to check if some condition is met before executing some code. In most programming and scripting languages today, the structure for doing this conditional check is the `if condition` check. This is also the case for Vim. In Vim scripting, the simplest format for expressing this is as follows:

```
if condition
    code-to-execute-if-condition-is-met
endif
```

If the `condition` evaluates to true, then the code between the `if` and the `endif` lines is executed. If the condition evaluates to false, then the code is not executed.

So, what can we use as condition in this `if` construct? There at two types of conditions you can use here—conditions using logic operators or string operators. So, let's take a look at how these operators look. In general, the format is:

```
value1 OPERATOR value2
```

Here, `OPERATOR` is the operator that compares `value1` with `value2`. An example could be:

```
value1 >= value2
```

This evaluates to true if `value1` is higher than or equal to `value2`. This is just one of the logical operators available. The following is a full list of the logical operators:

- `val1 == val2`: True if `val1` equals to `val2`
- `val1 != val2`: True if `val1` is not equal to `val2`
- `val1 > val2`: True if `val1` is higher than `val2`

- `val1 < val2`: True if `val1` is lower than `val2`
- `val1 >= val2`: True if `val1` is higher than or equal to `val2`
- `val1 <= val2`: True if `val1` is lower than or equal to `val2`

These operators can be used on both string values and numeric values because Vim can automatically convert back and forth between those types. In the case of strings, the operators work on the letters of the string one by one to see if their ASCII value is higher, lower, or equal to the one in the other string. For example, `"bbb">"aaa"` is true whereas `"abc">"abd"` is false (because c has a lower ASCII value that d).

When you work only with strings, there are some more conditions you would want to have available. These are the partial matches that you would want to use if you want to check whether a string contains a certain substring or character. In Vim, the operators for this look like this:

- `str1 =~ str2`: True if `str1` contains the `str2` substring or is equal to `str2`
- `str1 !~ str2`: True if `str1` does not contain, and is not equal to the `str2` substring

When using these operators, `str2` is typically a pattern and can use Vim's regular expressions (see `:help regexp` for more information). This means that you cannot only match simple strings, but can actually do advanced matches.

All these conditional operators can be used in the `if` construct and as you will see later, they can also be used elsewhere.

Let's look at some other cases where conditions are useful and can help make your code more structured.

In some cases, you might want to execute one piece of code if the condition evaluates to true, but another piece of code if it evaluates to false. Here, you could have two `if` conditions—one checking if the condition is true, and one checking if the condition is false. There is, however, another method.

With the `if-else-endif` construction, you can do just that. The format for expressing this in Vim scripting is as follows:

```
if condition
    code-to-execute-if-condition-is-true
else
    code-to-execute-if-condition-is-NOT-true
endif
```

Another case could be when you have a range of conditions and depending on which one evaluates to true, the correct piece of code should be executed. This could be done with the following:

```
if condition1
    code-to-execute-if-condition1-is-true
else
    if condition2
       code-to-execute-if-condition2-is-true
    endif
endif
```

As you can see, only one of `condition1` and `condition2` can be evaluated as true, but both can be evaluated as false. However, this code is cluttered and the extra `endif` can lead to incorrectly-ended `if` constructs if placed incorrectly.

A better way to write this is with the if-elseif-else construct, which is formatted as follows:

```
if condition1
    code-to-execute-if-conition1-is-true
elseif condition2
    code-to-execute-if-condition2-is-true
endif
```

This code does exactly the same as the previous example, except that it is a lot more readable. You can have more than one `elseif`, which means that you can have multiple conditions in the same structure without problems.

Later, when we come to working with loops, we will see how conditions can also be used there.

Working with lists and dictionaries

Previously, we have looked at how to create lists and dictionaries. Now, let's move on a bit and look at how to use the data we have stored in them.

When you have a list variable and you want to use one of the values it contains, you simply have to use the name of the variable with square brackets after it and with the index of the value you want. Index means the place in which the item is placed in the list, starting with first item being placed at index 0. So, if we want to echo the `"three"` value from the following list:

```
:let mylistvar1 = [1,2,"three",0x04, myfivevar]
```

It has index 2 and hence could be done like this:

```
:echo mylistvar1[2]
```

If we have a list of lists such as `mylistvar2`:

```
:let mylistvar2 = [[1,2,3],["four","five","six"]]
```

and want to echo the `"four"` value, then we need to access the index 0 of the inner list which is placed at index 1 of the outer list. This is done with:

```
:echo mylistvar2[1][0]
```

A point to note about lists in Vim is the possibility to use negative indices. Whenever a negative index is used, it will count from the back rather than from the front. So, to echo the `four` value from `mylistvar2`, it would look like this:

```
:echo mylistvar2[-1][-3]
```

Notice that -0 does not exist and hence the last item in a list is index -1.

> If you try to access a non-existing index of a list, Vim will give you an error. You can prevent this error from showing up by using the `get()` function instead, `:echo get(mylistvar1, 2)` where 2 is the index you want to try to access.

If you want to add another item to an already existing list in Vim, you have multiple choices. The simple way to do it is by using the `add()` function. An example of how this works is as follows:

```
:let mylistvar3 = [1,2,3,4]
:call add(mylistvar3, 5)
:echo mylistvar3
```

This adds the item "5" to the list and then prints the entire list, which now holds five items. Another way to do it is to use the list concatenation functionality in Vim. To concatenate two lists in Vim, you just have to use the + operator. An example of this is as follows:

```
:let mylistvar4 = [1,2,3,4]
:let mylistvar4 = mylistvar4 + [5,6,7,8]
:echo mylistvar4
```

This creates a list with four items (values 1-4), takes its value list and concatenates it with another list (containing the values 5-8), and then puts the concatenated list back into the `mylistvar4` variable. Finally, it echoes the list, which is now eight items long.

Instead of concatenating list one with list two before putting the value back into list one, you can do the entire thing in one move by using the combined equal operator, +=. This takes the right-hand side of the operator and adds it (concatenates) to the left-hand side. For example:
```
:let mylistvar4 += [5,6,7,8]
```

If the list you concatenate with is only one item, then it basically works like using the add function.

Besides using the + operator for concatenation, you can also use the extend() function. An example of how this works could look as follows:

```
:let mylistvar5 = [1,2,3,4]
:call extend(mylistvar5, [5,6,7,8])
:echo mylistvar5
```

Note that there is a very big difference between using the add() and extend() functions for adding elements to the list. If instead of using extend() you used add() in the previous command, then you would have added a list in the list resulting in mylistvar5. This looks like the following:

```
mylistvar5 = [1,2,3,4,[5,6,7,8]]
```

This only has five items, the fifth of which is a list containing another four items.

To remove an item from a list, you do it as if you were adding an item to the list. But now the function name is remove(). For example:

```
:call remove(mylistvar5, 3)
```

This removes the item with index 3 from the list in mylistvar5.

So, let's move on and look at how we can access and modify a dictionary variable. Previously, we created a dictionary variable looking like this:

```
:let mydictvar1 = {1: "one", 2: "two", 3: "three"}
```

Accessing this particular dictionary actually looks very much like accessing a list. If, for instance, we want to have the "two" value from the dictionary, we use the [ ] appended to the end again as with the lists:

```
:echo mydictvar1[2]
```

This looks a lot like the list we accessed, but notice what happens if we change the keys in the dictionary from numbers to some string:

```
:let mydictvar4 = {'banana': 'yellow', 'apple': 'green'}
```

And now, we want to access it again to get the color of the apple:

```
:echo mydictvar4['apple']
```

This will print the word `'green'` to the screen. An alternative way to do the same if your key is all alphabetic (ASCII) letters, numbers, or underscores is the following:

```
:echo mydictvar4.apple
```

The first character of the key must always be an ASCII letter.

So, compared to the list where everything was ordered and every item had an index, the directory is unordered and the key from the key-value pair is used to get the value instead of the index.

To change one of the values in the directory variable, you just use the following:

```
:let mydictvar4['apple'] = 'red'
```

To add another item to the dictionary, you do exactly as in the previous example, except that you use a key that is not already there in the dictionary.

As something special, you can attach a function to the dictionary variable and use it to make distinct things on or with the contents of the dictionary variable. This is better explained with an example, so let's see how that works.

Say, we want to be able to take a number and convert each of its digits into the same number written with letters. Let's call the `convert` function and the dictionary variable it is attached to so that it looks like this:

```
let mynumbers = {0:'zero',1:'one',2:'two',3:'three',4:'four',
                 5:'five',6:'six',7:'seven',8:'eight',9:'nine'}
```

The function could look like this:

```
function mynumbers.convert(numb) dict
    return join(map(split(a:numb,'\zs'),'get(self, v:val, "unknown")'))
endfunction
```

If we look at the function, there are a couple of things you need to notice.

The first thing is that this function is built like a normal function, except that the function name contains the name of your dictionary variable and we have the `dict` keyword after the function argument.

This keyword is what tells Vim that it should treat this function as a dictionary function and open up for the usage of a special variable—`self`. From now on, the `self` variable refers to the dictionary to which this function is bound. This means that we could basically do `self[1]` to get the value `"one"` and so on. The contents of the function itself are a combination of four functions:

- `split`: Splits the argument stored in `a:numb` into an unnamed list. For example:

```
:let a = split("one two")
:echo a;     " this prints "one"
```

- `map`: Maps a given command to every element in a list (the one from split). For example:

```
:let mylist = ["one", "two", "three"]
:call map(mylist, "<" . v:val . ">")
:echo mylist[0]     " this prints <one>
```

- `get`: Gets value from `self` where key is equal to `v:val` (value from `map`). For example:

```
:let mylist2 = ["one","two", "three"]
:echo get(mylist2, 2,"none") " prints three
:echo get(mylist2, 3, "none")   " prints "none"
```

- `join`: Joins all the elements returned by the map-get combination. For example:

```
:let mylist3 = ["one", "two", "three"]
:let mystring = join(mylist3, "+")
:echo mystring    " prints one+two+three
```

(See `:help split()`, `:help join()`, `:help map()`, `:help get()` for more information.)

So translated into a more understandable description, the `mynumbers.convert` function takes a range of digits (`a:numb`) and splits it into individual digits. It then uses each digit as a key to look up the value in the dictionary variable (`mynumbers`, known as `self`), joins all the returned values into a string by putting a whitespace between the values, and finally the string is returned.

So, now you can use your dictionary variable as a converter from numbers to written number names like this:

```
:echo mynumbers.convert(12345)
```

This prints "one two three four five", which is the `12345` argument in words. This is a functionality that opens up a lot of new possibilities.

Loops

When you are working with lists and dictionaries, it is often a needed functionality to be able to go through some or all of the items in the list / dictionary. For this a programmer would typically use loops, and this is also the case in Vim.

In Vim you have two available looping types:

- For loop
- While loop

In the next sections, we will look at how to work with these loops.

For loops

Let's start by taking a look at the `for` loop in different situations.

The `for` loop can be constructed in several different ways, of which this is the simplest:

```
for var in range
    do-something
endfor
```

In this case, we go through all values one by one and for each one of them, the `myvar` variable is updated to hold the value. An example could be:

```
for myvar in range(1,10)
    echo myvar
endfor
```

This uses the `range()` function to construct a range of numbers from 1 to 10 and then the `for` loop goes through them beginning with 1. The `myvar` variable will be updated for each iteration with the value found at the current number from the range. After executing this `for` loop, it will have printed the numbers 1 through 10.

This does not use a list, but can easily be changed so that it does. So, let's look at how that is constructed:

```
for var in list
    do-somthing
endfor
```

This is very simple, but let's look at an example to see how it works:

```
let mylist = ['a','b','c','d','e','f','g','h','i','j','k']
for itemvar in mylist
    echo itemvar
endfor
```

After executing this, it will have printed the letters a through k one by one. And there really isn't more to it when using a list.

When you use dictionaries, it takes a bit more work to get the values printed. This is because the value is bound to a key and not to an index. But we have a helper function that just extracts the keys from the dictionary and serves them to the for loop as if they were a list. The function's name is keys(). So, let's take a look at how we can use this in a for loop:

```
let mydict = {a: "apple", b:"banana", c: "citrus" }
for keyvar in keys(mydict)
    echo mydict[keyvar]
endfor
```

In this case, we get a list of keys from the mydict dictionary. We go through them one by one, giving keyvar the value of the current key. The value of keyvar is then used to look up the matching value in the mydict dictionary.

As the items in a dictionary are not ordered, in the previous example you could end up getting the values printed as banana citrus apple. There is, however, a function that will help you sort the keys and hence put the values in order. You simply have to use the sort() function on the list you get out of the keys() function.

```
let mydict = {a: "apple", b:"banana", c: "citrus" }
for keyvar in sort(keys(mydict))
    echo mydict[keyvar]
endfor
```

This, of course, requires that the names of the keys can be ordered individually by using a normal sort algorithm. In the previous case, there is no problem because a is before b, which is before c.

The sort function can actually take another argument, which is a function name. This way you can make your own sort algorithm to use when sorting special values. See :help sort() for more information and an example.

While loops

The next type of loop we will look at is the `while` loop. This type of loop, as the name indicates, runs for as long as some condition is true (remember how we previously defined what a condition is in the *Conditions* section). The basic construction for a while loop is as follows:

```
while condition
    execute-this-code
endwhile
```

Here, the code between the `while` and the `endwhile` lines is executed as long as the condition evaluates to true. So, let's look at an example of how that could work:

```
let x=0
while x <= 5
    echo "x is now " x
    let x+=1
endwhile
```

This example defines a variable x with the value of 0 and then goes into a loop that runs as long as x is lower than 5. For each iteration in the loop, it prints the value of x and then increments the value of x by 1. This will result in Vim printing:

```
x is now 0
```

```
x is now 1
```

```
x is now 2
```

```
x is now 3
```

```
x is now 4
```

```
x is now 5
```

When you use a while loop, there are some extra features available by using some specific statements inside the loop scope.

The first statement is the *break*, which makes the loop end right where it is, and Vim then jumps to the line right after the `endwhile`. An example could be:

```
let x=0
let y = 1000
while x <= 1000
    let y -= 10
    if y <= x
        break
    endif
    let x += 1
endwhile
```

This creates two variables x and y, and gives them the values 0 and 1000. Then it goes into a while loop where it subtracts 10 from the y for each loop iteration. And now the break statement comes into the picture because we now check with an if condition to see if the y variable is smaller than or equal to the x variable. If this is the case, we don't want to loop anymore and call the break. This ends the loop and takes us to just after the loop.

The second statement you can use in the while loop is the continue statement.

This statement takes you back to the while line in the while loop without executing the remaining lines under it.

An example of this could be the following:

```
let x=0;
while x <= 5
  let x+=1
    if x == 2
        continue
    endif
    echo "x is now " x
endwhile
```

This example basically loops x through the values 1-5. We want it to print out the value of x every time, except when x equals 2. So, in order to leave out the loop iteration where x equals 2, we check to see what the value is, and if it is 2, then we use the continue statement.

The output from this will be:

x is now 1

x is now 3

x is now 4

x is now 5

And that's all you need to know about loops to get you started with writing your own scripts.

> The break and continue statements can also be used in the for loop in the same way as shown in the examples with the while loop.

Creating functions

Throughout this book, we have already used different pieces of code that were constructed as a Vim function. We have, however, never actually gotten to look into how to actually construct a function and what exactly a function is.

Let's start by looking at the structure of a simple function:

```
function Name(arg1, arg2,...argN) keyword
    code-to-execute-when-function-is-called
endfunction
```

The `Name` is the name you want to call your function. It has to start with a capital letter and can only contain letters, numbers, and underscores.

The `arg1-argN` are arguments that the user of the function is required to give when calling the function. If you don't need any arguments from the user, then you can simply leave them out (having an empty `()` after the function name). You can have as many as 20 arguments for a function in Vim, and simply name them as you would like them to be used later in the code inside the function.

After the argument parentheses, it is possible to add a keyword that tells Vim something about what this function is used to do and how it should call it. We have already seen in this book that the keyword can have the following values:

- `Dict`: Tell Vim that this function is bound to a dictionary (covered in this chapter)
- `Range`: Tell Vim that this function is called once for a range of lines and not once for each line it is called on (Chapter 5, *Advanced Formatting*, when learning to create lists)

However, in most cases, you do not need this keyword and hence you can just leave it out.

Inside the function, you have all the code that you want executed when the function is called. All variables in this code are local to the function and will not be reachable later when the function has finished executing. If you need to use a variable from outside the function, you can either get it into the function as an argument, or you can use the variable name directly inside the function by adding the global scope marker `g:` to the variable name.

If you get a variable into a function as an argument, then the value is merely copied into the function, and the variable outside the function will not be updated when the value is changed inside the function.

The variables that you get into the function as an argument will have the scope marker a: in front of the name when used in the code.

Here is an example of how a simple function could look that takes two arguments and prints their sum:

```
function PrintSum(num1, num2)
    let sum = a:num1 + a:num2
    echo "the sum is ".sum
endfunction
```

This shows how to use the arguments in the function, but you might also want to be able to update a global variable with the sum. So, let's update the example to do this:

```
let sum = 0
function PrintSum(num1, num2)
    let sum = a:num1 + a:num2
    echo "the sum is ".sum
    let g:sum = sum
endfunction
```

Now, you can still use the sum variable after the function has ended. Let's say you did this:

```
let sum = 1
call PrintSum(4,5)
echo sum
```

Then this will print the value 9 since the PrintSum function has updated the global sum variable.

Updating global variables directly is, however, not considered a good programming practice and Vim also gives you another way of updating the global variable – the return statement.

The `return` statement makes the function return a value and end the execution of the function whenever Vim hits the statement. The returned value can then be assigned to the `sum` global variable directly when the function is called. So, let's once again update our example to use the `return` statement:

```
function PrintSum(num1, num2)
    let sum = a:num1 + a:num2
    echo "the sum is " sum
    return sum
endfunction
```

Now, you can change the function call to be as follows:

```
let sum = PrintSum(4,5)
echo sum
```

If the function had additional lines after the line with the `return` statement, they would never be executed because the function finishes execution after returning. This also means that you can only return one value from a function.

> You can have multiple `return` statements in your function, but the function will return when the first one is reached. However, some consider multiple return points to be a bad programming practice, unless it is not possible to get around without making the code less understandable.

Variable argument list

In the previous example, we only had two arguments for the functions. But what if you wished to calculate the sum of more than just those two? In Vim, you can have a variable length argument list by defining your function to have ... as the last argument in the argument list.

So, let's rewrite our `sum` function once again to take as many arguments as you like (but at least two to have something to sum):

```
function PrintSum(num1, num2,...)
    let sum = a:num1 + a:num2
    let argnum = 1
    while argnum <= a:0
        let sum += a:{argnum}
        let argnum+=1
    endwhile
    echo "the sum is " sum
    return sum
endfunction
```

This new function introduces some new variables.

The `argnum` is a counter that we use to go through all the arguments after the `num1` and `num2`.

The number of arguments that the function has been given is stored in the special variable `a:0`. So we use this as a stop for our `argnum` counter when we increase it.

To access each of the variables, we now use our `argnum` variable value as index to look up the argument in the list of optional arguments by using the `a:{argnum}` variable. You can see the `a:{}` as a list of the optional arguments (those after `num2`) given to the function, and then `argnum` is used as the index to look up.

For each extra argument in the argument list, we add the value to our sum and when done, we print the sum and return the value to the global scope.

This means that now we can do:

```
let sum = 0
let sum = PrintSum(4,5,6)
echo sum
let sum = PrintSum(4,5,6,5,4,3,2,1)
echo sum
let sum = PrintSum(1234,5432,3333)
echo sum
```

The result of this will be the following values:

15

30

9999

If you would rather have all the optional arguments as a list variable in the function, then Vim has another special variable called `a:000`, which acts as a list. With this, we can rewrite our function to look like this:

```
function PrintSum(num1, num2,...)
    let sum = a:num1 + a:num2
    for arg in a:000
        let sum += arg
    endfor
    echo "the sum is " sum
    return sum
endfunction
```

This time the values of the optional arguments are passed into the `arg` variable one by one in the `for` loop, and then we use the `arg` variable to add to the sum.

When you have created a function but do not want to use it anymore, you can remove it from your Vim session by using this command:

```
:delfunction function-name
```

Here, `function-name` is the name of the function you want to delete.

> To see what a function does, you can use the `:function` command to show it to you. In case of the previous example, you could use: `:function PrintSum`. If you leave out the function name, you will instead get a list of all available functions.

Besides the functions you create yourself, Vim also comes pumped full of functions for miscellaneous tasks. You can read more about the different functions in the help system under this:

```
:help 'function-list'
```

Summary

This chapter was especially meant for those who wanted to learn how to extend Vim with scripts. It started out with one of the simplest types of scripts for Vim—the syntax schemes. We learned how to create a syntax file for programming languages (or other syntactic contents) such that we can get some nice coloring of the contents.

After this, we moved on and looked at how one actually uses scripts in Vim. This was done by looking at the different types of script that are available for Vim and where to find them. We ended this session by looking at not only how to install Vim scripts, but also how to uninstall them again afterwards—a functionality, it turns out you can only easily use after installing a script in Vim.

So at this point, we knew how to install and use scripts, and it was time to move on to the actual development of scripts for Vim.

We started out by looking at the basic types in Vim and learned that Vim is nearly typeless (only two basic types). There were, however, many types of variables, and these are really useful for storing all the data needed when creating scripts.

So now, we knew about most of the basic structures of the Vim scripting language, and it was time to learn how to create functions.

We learned that by the use of a single keyword, Vim can be told how to call the function. This made it possible for us to bind a function to, for example, a dictionary variable. Thereby, we could have some extra functions that work directly on the contents of the dictionary.

With all this in hand, you are now ready to proceed to the next chapter where we will take a look at how you put it all together as a well-structured script file.

7
Extended Vim Scripting

In the previous chapter, we learned the basics of how to write a script for Vim. It is now time to learn how to put it all together in a structured manner and test your script.

This chapter will contain recipes focusing on the following subjects:

- How to structure a Vim script
- Tips for when you develop Vim scripts
- How to debug a Vim script
- How to use other scripting languages when writing Vim scripts

After you have read this chapter, you should be able to write your own scripts for Vim in both Vim script language and other languages. This means that you are now ready to extend the functionality of Vim.

Script structure

We have been through all the basics of Vim scripting, so now let's take a look at how to put it all together to form a complete script.

Since a Vim script is often just a single file, let's take this as being the goal of our example too. We also want to prepare the script for being made available to others and hence make the code very readable.

In the following sections, we will outline each of the elements of a well-formatted script.

Script header

A script should preferably always begin with a header that states what this script is all about. A script header should contain the following details:

- Who the maintainer is (you)
- The version when it was last updated
- A notice about which license you have released the script under (most importantly)

This could look like:

```
" myscript.vim   : Example script to show how a script is structured.
" Version        : 1.0.5
" Maintainer     : Kim Schulz<kim@schulz.dk>
" Last modified  : 01/01/2007
" License        : This script is released under the Vim License.
```

Notice how each line is prepended with a ". This means that the line is a comment from the quote until the end of the line.

Other information could be placed in the header, like maybe that the script depends on another script, or needs to be used with at least some specific Vim version.

Script-loaded check

It is always a good practice to check if the script has already been loaded once, and if it has, then unload the functions before moving on. This is good because the script is not only installed globally on the system but also in the user's own VIMHOME.

An example on how to check if a script has already been loaded could look like this:

```
if exists("loaded_myscript")
    finish "stop loading the script
endif
let loaded_myscript=1
```

If the script has never been loaded, the if condition will be false and we will go on and set the loaded_myscript variable.

The next time we try to load the script, the if condition will evaluate to true because loaded_myscript now exists and the script will then stop loading.

In some cases, it is not the best choice to just stop loading the script, because the user might have changed the version of the script in his or her VIMHOME. So instead of just calling finish, you could instead unload the functions and then just let the script create the functions again. The code to do this looks like the following:

```
if exists("loaded_myscript")
    delfunction MyglobalfunctionB
    delfunction MyglobalfunctionC
endif
let loaded_myscript=1
```

As you don't know if the user is in a compatible mode (more like vi, less like Vim), it is a good idea to store the user's compatible mode, while in your script. This makes it possible for your script to use Vim-specific functionality without problems. Add the following after the loaded check:

```
:let s:global_cpo = &cpo    " store current compatible-mode
                            " in local variable
:set cpo&vim                " go into nocompatible-mode
```

And then in the end of your script you set it all back as before:

```
:let &cpo = s:global_cpo
```

Script configuration

As other users open the script and start looking at it from the top, this is a good place to put all configurable settings. This can be things such as path to external programs, names of specific files the script needs, file types it should work on, and so on.

A user of the script might want to change the settings in his or her vimrc file, and you should therefore make sure that you do not overwrite his or her settings. This can be done by checking that the setting does not already exist and only setting it if it doesn't.

An example of settings for this script could be:

```
" variable myscript_path
if !exists("myscript_path")
    let s:vimhomepath = split(&runtimepath,',')
    let s:myscript_path = s:vimhomepath[0]."/plugin/myscript.vim"
else
    let s:myscript_path = myscript_path
    unlet myscript_path
```

```
endif

" variable myscript_indent
if !exists("myscript_indent")
    let s:myscript indent = 4
else
    let s:myscript_indent = myscript_indent
    unlet myscript_indent
endif
```

The example sets two configuration variables—`myscript_path` and `myscript_indent`. We check to see if the variable exists, and if it does not, then we set the default value in the script-scope variable name (for example, `s:myscript_path`).

If the user has already set this variable, then the value is assigned to the script-scope variable of the same name.

Finally, the user-defined variable is removed with `unlet`, so it does not float around in global scope with no purpose—configuration is only needed in the script and not in the global scope.

Key mappings

Now it is time to add your key mappings, if your script needs any. These could be for calling functions, setting variables, and other things. As with configuration variables, mappings is an area where the user might not want the same settings like you—or maybe some other script has already made the same mappings that you want. So let's look at a mapping example with a check to see if a mapping already exists:

```
if !hasmapto('<Plug>MyscriptMyfunctionA')
    map <unique> <Leader>a <Plug>MyscriptMyfunctionA
endif
```

We have several different pieces put together here when we construct the mapping and mapping check:

- `hasmapto()`: Function to check if a mapping to your function exists.
- `<unique>`: This tells Vim that it should give an error if a similar map exists.
- `<Leader>`: Lets the user decide which map leader to use. `<Leader>` is replaced by the contents of the global variable `mapleader`.
- `<Plug>`: This is a way to make a unique global identifier for a function, such that it will not clash with other functions in the global scope.

After putting it all together, we have created a check to see if some mapping is already made to the unique function identifier `<Plug>MyscriptMyfunctionA`. If a map does not exists, then `<Leader>a` is mapped to the identifier — unless `<Leader>a` is already used and Vim instead gives an error.

But you may wonder how do we get from `<Plug>MyscriptMyfunctionA` to the actual function, `MyfunctionA()`, in the script. Well, we have to perform some extra mappings to get this done.

```
noremap <unique> <script> <Plug>MyscriptMyfunctionA <SID>MyfunctionA
noremap <SID>MyfunctionA :call <SID>MyfunctionA()<CR>
```

The first mapping maps our unique `<Plug>MyscriptMyfunctionA` identifier to `<SID>MyfunctionA`. We use `<SID>` here, because this little tag is exchanged with Vim's own unique ID for the current script, and this is needed if we want to make a global mapping to a function that is only available in the script scope (for example, `s:MyfunctionA`).

The second mapping binds the actual function (`<SID>MyfunctionA()`, which is `s:MyfunctionA()`) to the global mapping `<SID>MyfunctionA`.

So what actually happens is that when you press \a (having `mapleader` set to \), then your first mapping translates this into `<Plug>MyscriptMyfunctionA`. This is defined in the script and hence `<SID>` now has the right value. Therefore, `<Plug>MyscriptMyfunctionA` is again translated further into `<SID>MyfunctionA`, which is finally mapped into the actual call of the local function `s:MyfunctionA()`.

You might find this complicated and a bit too much, and you might be right with a relatively unique function name like `MyfunctionA()`. But what if the function was called `Add()`, `Delete()`, `Convert()`, or some other function name that many scripts could have implemented. In those cases, the function names would clash and Vim would not know which one to use. You could of course just give your functions some weird unique names, but that will in the end just make your script code cluttered and pollute the global scope with unnecessary functions.

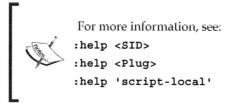

For more information, see:
`:help <SID>`
`:help <Plug>`
`:help 'script-local'`

Functions

The functions are probably the most important part. We have already seen how a function is created and noticed that it might be better than all functions that are not directly needed in the global scope and are added to the script scope with the `s:` scope marker. So an example of this could be:

```
" this is our local function with a mapping
function s:MyfunctionA()
    echo "this is the script-scope function MyfunctionA speaking"
endfunction


" this is a global function which can be called by anyone
function MyglobalfunctionB()
    echo "Hello from the global-scope function myglobalfunctionB"
endfunction
" this is another global function which can be called by anyone
function MyglobalfunctionC()
    echo "Hello from MyglobalfuncionC() now calling locally:"
    call <SID>MyfunctionA()
endfunction
```

The first function is a private function, which is only available in the script scope, while the other two are both available in the global scope. Notice, however, how it is possible for one of the global functions to call the local function because it knows the correct `<SID>` for the current script.

Putting it all together

If you have followed the description in the previous sections, you now have all you need in order to make a complete script.

So let's put it all together and see it as a full script example:

```
" myscript.vim  - Example script to show how a script is structured.
" Version       : 1.0.5
" Maintainer    : Kim Schulz<kim@schulz.dk>
" Last modified : 01/01/2007
" License       : This script is released under the Vim License.

" check if script is already loaded
if exists("loaded_myscript")
    finish "stop loading the script
endif
let loaded_myscript=1
```

```
      let s:global_cpo = &cpo   "store compatible-mode in local variable
      set cpo&vim               " go into nocompatible-mode
" ######## CONFIGURATION ########
" variable myscript_path
if !exists("myscript_path")
   let s:vimhomepath = split(&runtimepath,',')
   let s:myscript_path = s:vimhomepath[0]."/plugin/myscript.vim"
else
   let s:myscript_path = myscript_path
   unlet myscript_path
endif


" variable myscript_indent
if !exists("myscript_indent")
   let s:myscript_indent = 4
else
   let s:myscript_indent = myscript_indent
   unlet myscript_indent
endif


    " ######## FUNCTIONS #########
    " this is our local function with a mapping
function s:MyfunctionA()
   echo "This is the script-scope function MyfunctionA speaking"
endfunction

" this is a global function which can be called by anyone
function MyglobalfunctionB()
   echo "Hello from the global-scope function myglobalfunctionB"
endfunction
" this is another global function which can be called by anyone
function MyglobalfunctionC()
   echo "Hello from MyglobalfuncionC() now calling locally:"
   call <SID>MyfunctionA()
endfunction

" return to the users own compatible-mode setting
:let &cpo = s:global_cpo
```

And there you have it! Our very first Vim plugin script! It might not have that much functionality, but it shows very well how you should structure your script to make it more understandable. Vim has other types of scripts such as file type plugins, compiler plugins, and library scripts. You can read more about how to modify your script in order to make it like these types of scripts in:

```
:help 'write-filetype-plugin'
:help 'write-compiler-plugin'
:help 'write-library-script'
```

 On the Vim online community site, http://www.vim.org, you will find thousands of scripts, which you can use as inspiration. Some of these are even library scripts that add functions you can use in your own script to speed up development.

Scripting tips

In this section, we will look at a few extra tips that can be handy when you create scripts for Vim. Some are simple code pieces you can add directly in your script, while others are good-to-know tips.

Gvim or Vim?

Some scripts have extra features when used in the GUI version of Vim (Gvim). This could be adding menus, toolbars, or other things that only work if you are using Gvim. So what do you do to check if the user runs the script in a console Vim or in Gvim? Vim has already prepared the information for you. You simply have to check if the feature gui_running is enabled. To do so, you use a function called has(), which returns 1 (true) if a given feature is supported / enabled and 0 (false), otherwise.

An example could be:

```
if has("gui_running")
    "execute gui-only commands here.
endif
```

This is all you need to do to check if a user has used Gvim or not. Note that it is not enough to check if the feature "gui" exists, because this will return true if your Vim is just compiled with GUI support—even if it is not using it.

Look in `:help 'feature-list'` for a complete list of other features you can check with the `has()` function.

Which operating system?

If you have tried to work with multiple operating systems such as Microsoft Windows and Linux, you will surely know that there are many differences.

This can be everything from where programs are placed, to which programs you have available and how access to files is restricted.

Sometimes, this can also have an influence on how you construct your Vim script as you might have to call external programs, or use other functionality, specific for a certain operating system.

Vim lets you check which operation system you are on, such that you can stop executing your script or make decisions about how to configure your script. This is done with the following piece of code:

```
if has("win16") || has("win32") || has("win64")|| has("win95")
    " do windows things here
elseif has("unix")
    " do linux/unix things here
endif
```

This example only shows how to check for Windows (all flavors available) and Linux / Unix. As Vim is available on a wide variety of platforms, you can of course also check for these. All of the operating systems can be found in:

`:help 'feature-list'`

Which version of Vim?

Throughout the last decade or two, Vim has developed and been extended with a large list of functions. Sometimes, you want to use the newest functions in your script, as these are the best / easiest to use. But what about the users who have a version of Vim that is older than the one you use, and hence don't have access to the functions you use?

You have three options:

1. Don't care and let it be the user's own problem (not a good option).
2. Check if the user uses an old version of Vim, and then stop executing the script if this is the case.
3. Check if the user has too old a version of Vim, and then use alternative code.

The first option is really not one I would recommend anyone to use, so please don't use it.

The second option is acceptable, if you can't work around the problem in the old version of Vim. However, if it is possible to make an alternative solution for the older version of Vim, then this will be the most preferable option.

So let's look at how you can check the version of Vim.

Before we look at how to check the version, we have to take a look at how the version number is built.

The number consists of three parts:

- Major number (for example, 7 for Vim version 7)
- Minor number (for example, 3 for Vim version 6.3)
- Patch number (for example, 123 for Vim 7.0.123)

The first two numbers are the actual version number, but when minor features / patches are applied to a version of Vim, it is mostly only the patch number that is increased. It takes quite a bit of change to get the minor number to increase, and a major part of Vim should change in order to increase the major version number.

Therefore, when you want to check which version of Vim the user is using, you do it for two versions — major and minor versions and patch number. The code for this could look like:

```
if v:version >= 702 || v:version == 701 && has("patch123")
    " code here is only done for version 7.1 with patch 123
    " and version 7.2 and above
endif
```

The first part of the `if` condition checks if our version of Vim is version 7.2 (notice that the minor version number is padded with 0 if less than 10) or above. If this is not the case, then it checks to see if we have a version 7.1 with patch 123. If patch version 124 or above is included, then you also have patch 123 automatically.

Printing longer lines

Vim was originally created for old text terminals where the length of lines was limited to a certain number of characters. Today, this old limitation shows up once in a while.

One place where you meet this limitation of line length is when printing longer lines to the screen using the "echo" statement. Even though you use Vim in a window where there are more than the traditional 80 characters per line, Vim will still prompt you to press *Enter* after echoing lines longer than 80 characters. There is, however, a way to get around this, and make it possible to use the entire window width to echo on. Window width means the total number of columns in the Vim window minus a single character. So if your Vim window is wide enough to have 120 characters on each line, then the window width is 120-1 characters.

By adding the following function to your script, you will be able to echo screen-wide long lines in Vim:

```
" WideMsg() prints [long] message up to (&columns-1) length
function! WideMsg(msg)
    let x=&ruler | let y=&showcmd
    set noruler noshowcmd
    redraw
    echo a:msg
    let &ruler=x | let &showcmd=y
endfunction
```

 This function was originally proposed by the Vim script developer Yakov Lerner on the Vim online community site at http://www.vim.org.

Now whenever you need to echo a long line of text in your script, instead of using the echo statement you simply use the function WideMsg(). An example could be:

```
:call WideMsg("This should be a very long line of text")
```

The length of a single line message is still limited, but now it is limited to the width of the Vim window instead of the traditional 80-1 characters.

Debugging Vim scripts

Sometimes things in your scripts do not work exactly as you expect them to. In these cases, it is always good to know how to debug your script.

In this section, we will look at some of the methods you can use to find your error.

 Well-structured code often has fewer bugs and is also easier to debug.

In Vim, there is a special mode to perform script debugging. Depending on what you want to debug, there are some different ways to start this mode. So let's look at some different cases.

If Vim just throws some errors (by printing them at the bottom of the Vim window), but you are not really sure where it is or why it happens, then you might want to try to start Vim directly in debugging mode. This is done on the command line by invoking Vim with the -D argument.

```
vim -D somefile.txt
```

The debugging mode is started when Vim starts to read the first vimrc file it loads (in most cases the global vimrc file where Vim is installed). We will look at what to do when you get into debug mode in a moment.

Another case where you might want to get into debug mode is when you already know which function the error (most likely) is in, and hence, just want to debug that function. In that case you just open Vim as normal (load the script with the particular function if needed) and then use the following command:

```
:debug call Myfunction()
```

Here everything after the :debug is the functionality you want to debug. In this case, it is a simple call of the function Myfunction(), but it could just as well be any of the following:

```
:debug read somefile.txt
:debug nmap ,a :call Myfunction() <CR>
:debug help :debug
```

So let's look at what to do when we get into the debugging mode.

When reaching the first line that it should debug, Vim breaks the loading and shows something like:

```
Entering Debug mode.   Type "cont" to continue.
cmd: call MyFunction()
  >
```

Now you are in the Vim script debugger and have some choices for what to make Vim do.

 If you are not familiar with debugging techniques, it might be a good idea to read up on this subject before starting to debug your scripts.

The following commands are available in the debugger (shortcuts are in parentheses):

- `cont` (c): Continue running the scripts / commands as normal (no debugging) until the next breakpoint (more about this later).
- `quit` (q): Quit the debugging process without executing the last lines.
- `interrupt` (i): Stop the current process like `quit`, but go back to the debugger.
- `step` (s): Execute the next line of code and come back to the debugger when it is finished. If a line calls a function or sources a file, then it will step into the function / file.
- `next` (n): Execute the `next` command and come back to the debugger when it is finished. If used on a line with a function call, it does not go into the function but steps over it.
- `finish` (f): Continue executing the script without stopping on breakpoints. Go into debug mode when done.

So now you simply execute the different commands to go through the lines of the script / function to see how it jumps through the `if` conditions, and so on. If you want to execute the same command multiple times, you simply press *Enter* without feeding a new command.

You can at any point execute another `Ex` command if needed (see `:help 'ex-command-index'`), but note that you don't have direct access to the variables, among others, in the debugger, unless they are global.

Sometimes, the place you want to get to is many lines into the code, and you really don't want to step all the way through the code until you get to that place.

In that case, you can insert a breakpoint at the exact line where you want to start the real debugging, and then just execute a `cont` as the first command. A breakpoint is inserted by one of the following commands, depending on how you want it inserted:

```
breakadd func linenum functionname
breakadd file  linenum filename
breakadd here
```

The first example sets a breakpoint on a particular function. The `functionname` can be a pattern such as `Myfunction*` if you, for instance, want to break on any function with a name that begins with `Myfunction`.

Sometimes, however, it is not in a function that the problem resides, but rather around a specific line in a file. If this is the case, then you should use the second command, where you give it a line number and a filename pattern as arguments to tell it where to break.

The final command is used if you have already stepped to the right place in the file but want to be able to break on it the next time you go through the code in the debugger. This command simply sets a breakpoint on the current line, in the current file, where you currently are in the debugger.

You can at any point of time get a list of breakpoints with the following command:

`:breaklist`

If a breakpoint is no longer needed, you have to delete it. As when adding breakpoints, there are a few different ways to delete them also.

The simplest way to do it is by simply finding the number of the breakpoint in the list of breakpoints, and then using the following command:

`:breakdel number`

Alternatively, you can delete the breakpoints the same way as you added them — except that you now use `breakdel` instead of `breakadd`:

`:breakdel func linenum functionname`

`:breakdel file linenum file`

`breakdel here`

If you want to remove all breakpoints, you can do it in one step by using this command:

`:breakdel *`

You can add a breakpoint directly on the command line when going into debug mode. Simply use the -c argument as follows:

```
vim -D -c 'breakadd file 15 */.vimrc' somefile.txt
```

Distributing Vim scripts

Now that your script is ready, it is time for you to distribute the script (if you have chosen to do so). The online Vim community has become the de facto place to publish scripts for others to find. Because of this, I urge you to do the same. But before you get to this, there are a couple of things you have to get ready.

First of all, you need to figure out whether your script needs to be packed into a compressed file such as a ZIP file, or if it should just be distributed as a single .vim file. The main reason for choosing the first option is that your script consists of multiple files (such as main script, file type plugin, syntax file, documentation, and so on).

How to create ZIP files (or related file types) is beyond what this chapter will look at, but here are a couple of pointers on how I make my ZIP files "install ready":

- Create the ZIP file including the folders where the files are placed relative to your VIMHOME. For example, consider that you have:

  ```
  VIMHOME/plugin/myscript.vim
  VIMHOME/syntax/mylang.vim
  VIMHOME/doc/myscript.txt
  ```

  Then the ZIP file should contain the three folders: plugin, syntax, and doc with one file in each. This makes the installation easy, as you simply have to go into your VIMHOME and then unpack the ZIP file.

- Always include a help file for your script. This file should be installed in VIMHOME/doc/ and contain descriptions of what the script does, which settings it has, and how to use it.

Even though you only have one script file, it can still be a good idea to put it in a ZIP file together with a help file. This makes it easier for you to remember to add documentation. We will look more at how to create Vim documentation in the next section.

Making Vimballs

Another, maybe even more interesting, alternative is to make a Vimball. We have previously looked at how to use Vimballs to install scripts, so it could now be interesting to look a bit at how to create one.

The command to create a Vimball is constructed as:

`:[range]MkVimball filename.vba`

This sure seems simple, right? And it really is. There is, however, a bit of preparation you need to do before calling this function.

The first thing you have to do is to open a new empty buffer in Vim with:

`:enew`

Now you add the paths to all the files (one on each line) relative to your VIMHOME. Considering the previous ZIP file example, it could look like:

```
plugin/myscript.vim
doc/myscript.txt
syntax/mylang.vim
```

When this is done you are actually ready to execute the command across the range of lines. Place the cursor on the first line in the buffer, go into normal mode, and use the keys *Shift+v* to select all the lines with paths on. Now all you have to do is execute the command:

`:MkVimball myscript.vba`

Vim will automatically add the range of the lines you have selected in front of the command. The filename `myscript.vba` can be any name, but if the file already exists, then a warning is given, but no file is written.

If you really want to overwrite an existing file, then just add an `!` after the `MkVimball` command to tell Vim that you mean it. There is no more to it. You now have a Vimball file called `myscript.vba`, which can be installed as described earlier in this chapter.

Remember that you need to install the Vimball script in order to use the Vimball functions we have described at. The latest version of the Vimball script can always be found here: `http://www.vim.org/scripts/script.php?script_id=1502`.

Remember the documentation

Vim has a very comprehensive help system with help for nearly any aspect of using Vim. But what happens when a user installs your script and wants to find "help" about it? If you haven't added documentation with your script installation, then the user will be out of luck and find no help in the help system. But why not follow the good concept that Vim has started about documenting everything? In other words: "Please include documentation when you release a script for Vim."

So let's take a look at how to create Vim documentation so that it has links, markers, tags, and so on, just like the real Vim documentation.

A Vim documentation document is just a plain text file with some special markup. When you create a new document, the first line is the most important of them all. So let's start by looking at that line:

```
*docname.txt* single line of description
```

The first * should be the very first character on the very first line of the file.

The `docname.txt` is the name of the file you are currently editing. Vim uses this when linking to the file from the "local additions" list in the Vim help system (see `:help local-additions`). The description after the second * is a one-line description of what this document is all about. In the case of our example, this line could be:

```
*myscript.txt* Documentation for example script myscript.vim
```

After this line, you place the actual contents of the document.

Typically, this starts with a longer description of what this document is about, and what it will explain. This could include your name and contact information (e-mail address, home page, and so on). After that, a table of contents could be added if the document is long enough to need one (we add it here as an example). It could, in the case of `myscript.vim`, look like this (including the first line):

```
*myscript.txt* Documentation for example script myscript.vim

Script : myscript.vim - Example script for vim developers
Author : Kim Schulz
Email  : <kim@schulz.dk>
Changed: 01/01/2007
=============================================================
                                              *myscript-intro*

1. Overview~
```

```
This document gives a short introduction to the example
script myscript.vim.
This script is made as an example for vim users on how to
structure a simple vim plugin script such that it is easy
to read and figure out.
The following is covered in this document:

    1. Overview             |myscript-intro|
    2. Mappings             |myscript-mappings|
    3. Functions            |myscript-functions|
    4. Todo                 |myscript-todo|

=============================================================
```

In this example, we use most of the formatting tags you have available for Vim documents. Let's go through them one by one to see what they mean.

The first markup is the *...*, which marks keywords that the Vim help system can jump to. In this case, we have *myscript-intro*, which makes it possible to jump directly to this section in the documentation with:

`:help 'myscript-intro'`

The next quite simple marker is ~ after the Overview headline. This marks the line with a different color from the rest of the text.

Then we come to |...| around some keywords next to each item in the table of contents. This creates a link to a particular section with a matching keyword (marked with *...*). The lines with equal signs are just a good way to mark section borders; they are not actually a markup type.

The following sections would be formatted in the same way, except if they had a part that shows a piece of Vim code. In that case, another markup would be used. An example of this could be in the function section. So let's take that as an example:

```
=============================================================
                                        *myscript-functions*
3. Functions~
Besides the functions available via mappings (as described
in |myscript-mappings|) there are some extra global func-
tions available.

MyglobalfunctionB()~
This function is one of the global functions in this script.
An example of usage could be: >
        :call MyglobalfunctionB()
    <
```

```
    Vim returns:
     Hello from the global-scope function myglobalfunctionB~


MyglobalfunctionC()~
This function is a global function that also calls one of
the internal functions ("s:MyfunctionA()") in the script.
An example of usage could be: >
     :call MyglobalfunctionC()
<
     Vim returns:
     Hello from MyglobalfuncionC() now calling locally:~
     This is the script-scope function MyfunctionA speaking~
================================================================
```

The special markup in this section is the >...< around the code examples. This is used to mark the code, while we use the ~ colored lines to mark the return from Vim.

That is basically all you need to know in order to create readable documentation for your script.

When the user wants to install the documentation, he or she places it in VIMHOME/doc/ and then he or she uses the following command:

:helptags docdir

Here docdir is the path to VIMHOME/doc/. If any of the keywords you have added are already used, then Vim will give you a warning, and you have to change it before distributing the documentation.

Want to distribute your documentation in multiple languages? Take a look in the help system for more information:
:help 'help-translated'.

Using external interpreters

Even though you can do nearly everything with Vim scripts, there are, however, some things that might be smarter or faster to do in other languages. The developers of Vim have recognized this need, and therefore implemented the possibility to interface with other scripting languages from within Vim. There are in particular three languages that you have access to:

- Perl
- Python
- Ruby

In the following sections, will we take a peek at how to interface with these scripting languages and which variables you have access to.

The support for these language interfaces is not included in Vim by default, and you will have to either compile Vim yourself to get it, or find a precompiled version that supports them.

To check if your version supports one of the languages, you simply run Vim on the command line with -version argument:

```
vim -version
```

Then, you look through the list of features to see if it has one of the following in the list:

```
+perl
```

```
+python
```

```
+ruby
```

It needs to say + in front of the language name to show that it is included. If it instead says, for example, -perl, then Perl support is not included.

Alternatively, you can just open up Vim and then test for the features with the has() function:

```
:echo has("perl")
```

```
:echo has("python")
```

```
:echo has("ruby")
```

It should return 1 for the languages you have support for.

Vim scripting in Perl

Perl is a very popular scripting language that has been around for quite some time now. It is very powerful when it comes to parsing text and other similar tasks. This also makes it very useful from within Vim.

The simplest way to use Perl in Vim is with the following command:

`:perl command`

This executes the Perl command in the argument `command`. Note that the values you set with the Perl command will persist throughout the entire Vim editing session.

Often you would, however, like to execute more than just a single command and hence you have to use another command.

In that case you can use:

```
:perl << endpattern
    perl code here
endpattern
```

This executes all the Perl code between the `endpattern` at the beginning and at the end.

> In Perl, Python, or Ruby, you can use anything for your `endpattern`, but the last one needs to be the only word on that particular line, and should be at the beginning of the line. If you leave out the first `endpattern`, then Vim defaults to use a single dot as `endpattern`.

An example that just prints a single line of text to Vim could be:

```
:perl << EOF
    VIM::Msg("this is a text");
EOF
```

Note how `EOF` is used as `endpattern`, and that in the Perl code I used a function called `VIM::Msg()` to print a message into Vim. This is just one among many functions you can use to interface between Vim and Perl. Other examples of Vim functions you can use from Perl are:

- `VIM::buffers()`: Return a list of all buffers open in Vim.
- `VIM::SetOption("option")`: Set a Vim option from Perl.
- `$curbuf->Name()`: Returns the name of the current buffer.
- `$curbuf->Set(100, "fooo")`: Replace line `100` in current buffer with new text.

- `$curwin->SetCursor(15,8)`: Set cursor at line 15, column 8 in current window.

You can find a full list of the Vim-specific functions you can use from within Perl by looking in the help system with:

`:help perl-pverview`

If you put Perl code in your script, you should always remember to check if the user has support for Perl in his or her version of Vim.

It is always a good idea to have your Perl code wrapped in Vim functions in your script. This way it is easy to implement your script, and for an inexperienced user, the script will look normal and work as usual. An example of how to wrap Perl in a function could be:

```
function MoveCursor(row,col)
    if has("perl")
        perl << EOF
        ($oldrow,$oldcol) = $curwin->Cursor();
        VIM::Msg("Old position was: ($oldrow,$oldcol)");
        $curwin->Cursor(row,col);
EOF
    else
        echo "perl not available. canceling function call"
    endif
endfunction
```

This function gets the old position of the cursor in the current window, prints that position, and then moves the cursor to the position that matches the two arguments for the function (row and column).

If the user does not have Perl support, then a message about this will be written. Note how the EOF is placed entirely to the left, even though the rest of the code is indented. This is strictly needed in order for Vim to be able to recognize it as the endpattern.

Vim scripting in Python

Through the recent years, Python has become the favorite scripting language for many programmers. This is mainly for its ease of use and strict rules about indenting (which lead to more readable code).

As with Perl, there is also an interface for Python in Vim, such that you can break out of Vim and use Python in your script. There are three main ways to use Python:

1. When you only want to execute a single Python statement from Vim:
   `:python statement`. An example could be:

   ```
   :python print "hello Vim developer"
   ```

2. If you want to execute a larger amount of Python code at the same time, you can use the following from Vim:

   ```
   :python << endpattern
        python statements here
   endpattern
   ```

   This executes all the Python code between the endpatterns.

3. The third option for using Python from within Vim is by executing an entire Python script file. This is done with the following command from Vim:

   ```
   :pyfile file.py
   ```

   Replace `file.py` with the name of the script you want to execute.

Sometimes your Python script expects to get some command-line arguments. It is, however, not possible to pass these in the `pyfile` command.

There is, however, a workaround where you set the arguments in `sys.argv` before executing the Python script file. An example could be:

```
:python import sys
:python sys.argv = ["argument1", "argument2"]
:pyfile myscript.py
```

To make it easier to interface between Python and Vim, there is a Python module available called vim. This module gives access to some extra functionality in Vim. Here is an example of usage in a Python script:

```
import vim
window = vim.current.window
window.height =200
window.width = 10
window.cursor = (1,1)
```

You can find a complete list of available functions in the help system in:

```
:help 'python-vim'
```

It is always a good idea to wrap your Python code into Vim functions if you use it in a Vim script.

Vim scripting in Ruby

For many programmers in the western world, Ruby has been an unknown language until just recently. It has, however, been quite a popular programming language in Asia for some time, and after its introduction as a scripting language for web development it has become quite popular in the rest of the world. A real strength of Ruby is said to be the fact that it is truly object oriented, which makes the language very modular.

Vim has a nice interface for Ruby, such that you can use it from within Vim. This can be done in several different ways. The simplest way to execute single Ruby commands in Vim is with the following: `:ruby command`.

Replace command with any single-line Ruby command. An example could be:

`:ruby print "Hello from Ruby"`

You might, however, want to execute several lines of Ruby in a sequence. This can be done with the following Vim command:

```
:ruby << endpattern
      ruby commands here
endpattern
```

This executes all the Ruby code between the endpatterns. If you set any variables or create any objects in the code, then these will be stored for later use in Vim.

Here is an example of what this could look like:

```
:ruby << EOF
   window = VIM::Window.current
   window.height = 250
   window.width = 35
   window.cursor = (10,10)
EOF
```

If your Ruby code is in a file, then you can even load this file directly in Vim and execute it. This is done with the following command:

`:rubyfile file.rb`

This is basically an alternative to using:

`:ruby load 'file.rb'`

Again all objects, among others, that you create in the script are stored in Vim for later usage, unless you remove them in the script.

To interface with Vim from your Ruby script, there is a Vim module available for Ruby. The module is called VIM and contains methods for a variety of Vim-related tasks.

Here are some examples of what it can be used for:

- `VIM::Set_option('option')`: Set a vim option
- `VIM::Message("message")`: Print a message in Vim
- `$curwin.height`: The height of the current window
- `$curbuf.width`: The width of the current buffer
- `VIM::Buffer.current.append(10, "line")`: Append a line to current buffer
- `VIM::Buffer.current.length`: Return the number of lines in current buffer

You can find a full list of available methods and objects in:

```
:help 'ruby-vim'
```

 Always remember to check if the user has Ruby available before using it in your script.

Summary

This chapter has been a chapter especially for those who wanted to learn how to create complete scripts for Vim.

Having learned about how the different parts of a script were constructed, it was time to see how we put it all together in a script. We took a top-down approach and went through a script example—line by line.

An important lesson learned was that a script programmer does not know how the user has his or her Vim configured and hence has to make sure that the correct settings exist and that the script does not break any of the users settings.

We learned how to use variables and functions that are only available in the scope of the script, such that we don't pollute the global scope with all our variables and functions. Again this was to help the user such that only the relevant functionality is available to him or her.

After looking at the structure of the script example, we ended the chapter with a couple of tips about how to make your script check for all sorts of things such as the operating system and the version of Vim.

Having created a script, it was time to learn how to debug it if something went wrong in the script. This took us through the debug mode in Vim and we learned how to step through the code line by line.

The script was ready and it was time to distribute it to others. We therefore took a look at how to distribute your script to others, such that they can also install and use it.

Documentation is an important part of a distributed script, so we looked at how the Vim documentation markup language works and how we can use it to create documentation for our script. Having documentation for our script also makes our script show up in the Vim help system under local additions. This makes it easy to jump directly to the documentation by the use of tags and keywords.

For some people, the Vim scripting language is not enough to satisfy all needs. Because of this, we looked at how to use external scripting languages from within Vim.

We looked at three languages, as these are some of the most popular ones available in Vim—Perl, Python, and Ruby. We noted that these external languages are not actually available in Vim by default, but had to be enabled at compile time. There are, however, precompiled versions of Vim available that contain these languages.

We went through the three different languages and learned how to execute a single command from the language, a range of commands, and in the case of Python and Ruby, even entire scripts.

We also learned that all of the languages have their own modules available such that they can interface with Vim. These modules give access to many of the functions you normally find in Vim and you can thereby control Vim directly from the script.

So that's it! After reading this, you should now be able to create your own well-structured, distributable Vim scripts and be able to debug them to find problems. You can now go on to the appendices and see what types of scripts other vim users have created in order to make Vim do nearly anything.

A
Vim Can Do Everything

It was once said that Vim can do everything. This might not be entirely true, but Vim can surely do a lot of different things that you might not have imagined it can.

In this appendix, we will take a look at some of the things that Vim users have made it do via Vim scripting or by combining it with other programs.

This appendix will take you through everything from games and mail clients, to IRC chatting and complete development IDE setups—all done in Vim.

Vim games

Even though Vim is a text editor, people have spent a lot of time on creating scripts that make it do other things (other than being an editor). Among these are small games that you can play directly inside the Vim editor. Notice that these are not just simple games like "20 questions" where everything can be done in text. These are actual graphical games! The graphics are not the best because they are created as so-called ASCII-art. They are, however, enough to give reasonably good game-play, and hours of fun.

So let's take a quick rundown on some of the games that Vim users have created for Vim in Vim script.

Game of Life

The first game is not really a game, but still a script worth mentioning. The Game of Life is what's normally called a zero-player-game because you don't play the game, but rather just watch how the game plays itself. The game has a simple artificial intelligence that emulates the evolution of cells. The cells follow some very basic rules:

1. Any living cell with fewer than two living neighbors dies, as if by loneliness.

2. Any living cell with more than three living neighbors dies, as if by overcrowding.

3. Any living cell with two or three living neighbors lives, and moves on as being the next generation.

4. Any dead cell with exactly three living neighbors comes to life.

In 1996, a guy who calls himself Eli the Bearded created a Vim script that implements these rules and prints a Game of Life in the current buffer. It was not particularly fast, but was meant as a proof-of-concept implementation. For most people this game will be quite boring, but for Game of Life enthusiasts, this implementation could be very interesting.

You can find the Game of Life at the following site: `http://www.vanhemert.co.uk/vim/vimacros/life1.vim`.

Nibbles

When I got my very first PC back in 1986, I only had one game to play. This was a game called Nibbles. I have spent a lot of time playing this game, where I had to control a small worm moving around, in different levels. In each level, it had to eat some things in order to grow. For each thing it ate, another part was added to the end of the worm, and after a while the worm was really long. You could not cross the boundaries or wall of the level and you were not allowed to cross your own tail as well.

In 2004, Hari Krishna Dara recreated this fine game as a Vim script. He only implemented a few levels, but made it possible to easily add more levels, if needed. The game-play was nice and it ran quite smoothly, if you keep in mind that it reprints parts of the text over and over again.

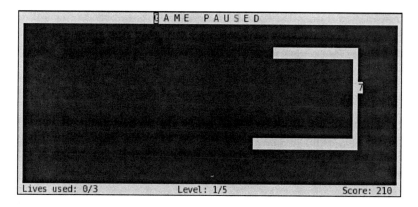

You can find the latest version of the game at the following address:
`http://www.vim.org/scripts/script.php?script_id=91`.

Rubik's cube

In 1974, a Hungarian sculptor and professor of architecture, Ernő Rubik created a complex mechanical cube consisting of 27 smaller cubes. The sides had different colors such that each face of the cube had the same color. However, if you turned the layers that the smaller cubes created, you could scramble the colors, and the puzzle of the game was to get it back into an unscrambled setup again.

In 2005, more than 30 years after the first Rubik's cube, Olivier Vermersch recreated the game of Rubik's cube in Vim script. The Vim version of the cube can still give the player hours of fun and mind puzzle.

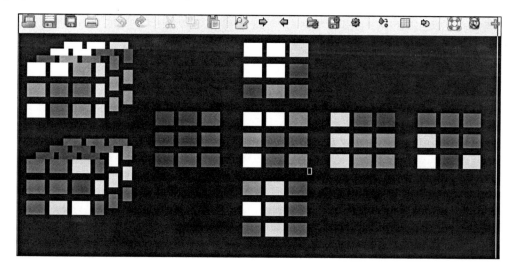

The script that makes it possible to play the game is available via the online Vim community. Instructions on how to download and play this game can be found at this address: http://www.vim.org/scripts/script.php?script_id=1271.

Tic-Tac-Toe

Most of the children of the modern world know the simple game of Tic-Tac-Toe and have played it at some point of their life. So, why not implement this game in Vim, such that you can play against your favorite editor to see which of you is the smarter one?

In 1996, Kevin Earls decided to do so, and this ended up as a list of Vim macros that combined to give a nice little Tic-Tac-Toe game inside a Vim buffer.

Even though the artificial intelligence for the opponent (Vim) is not that advanced, it can still be quite hard to win against.

You can find the script file you need to use, in order to get this game, at Mr. Earls' home page. Installation and usage instructions are inside the script:
http://www.vanhemert.co.uk/vim/vimacros/ttt.vim.

Mines

Back in 1995, when Microsoft released Windows 95, one of the games that came with it was a little game called Mines or Minesweeper. The game was a mixture of a simple numeric puzzle, and a gamble game. The player had to get an entire area cleared of mines, by either clicking on areas without mines (guessing) or calculating where the mines were, and marking them with a flag. To calculate the placement of the mines, you had to get an area cleared first. This revealed some numbers that said how many mines there were in the squares next to this particular area. When you calculate where a mine is placed, you mark it with a flag.

In 2004, Charles E. Campbell recreated this game in Vim script, such that you can get up a minefield in an empty Vim buffer. You can play the game in different difficulty levels. Although you can win the easy mode quite easily, you can get a headache while trying to get the mines marked on time in the higher levels.

You can find the script that makes this possible on the Vim online community by following this link: http://vim.sourceforge.net/scripts/script.php?script_id=551.

On this site, you will also find information about how to install and use this game.

Sokoban

I have to admit that I just love to play puzzle games, so I obviously also like the game Sokoban. The game play is simple and so is the user interface — however, the puzzles are mind-bending and quite hard. The task is to be a small man who has to move some boxes around in mazes / corridors. Sounds easy right? The man can however, only push and not pull the boxes. So, whenever it gets into a corner or blind alley, the box is stuck and you cannot get through that level without restarting.

In 2002, Mike Sharpe recreated this game in Vim using the level definitions from the old Linux game XSokoban. He kept the user interface very simple but the game play is still great.

 You can find the game XSokoban at the following address: http://www.cs.cornell.edu/andru/xsokoban.html.

If you want to play this fine game, then you can find the script and installation instructions on the Vim online community site at this address: http://www.vim.org/scripts/script.php?script_id=211.

Tetris

The final game for Vim that I am going to mention in this appendix is a real classic—Tetris, where blocks of different sizes and shapes fall down and need to be placed properly to produce complete rows. This game can be dated back to 1985; the Russian Alexey Pajitnov designed and created it. Since then, the game has been implemented for almost any platform, and in hundreds of different variations over the same theme.

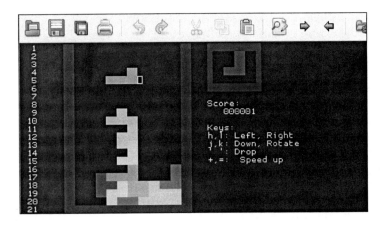

In 2002, Gergely Kontra decided to implement this game in Vim script and this turned into yet another fine implementation of this classic game. The game even has different modes and keeps a high-score list so that you can play against your own previous records.

You can find the game at the Vim online community site at the following address:
`http://www.vim.org/scripts/script.php?script_id-172`.

Here, you will also find instructions about installation and how to play.

Programmers IDE

Throughout this book, I have talked about features in Vim that could be used when you are a programmer, several times. Personally, I use Vim for nearly all the programming tasks that I do, but I am often met with skeptical comments from other programmers: "How can you use such a primitive editor?", "How can you live without an Integrated Development Environment (IDE)?", they say. Well, Vim can give you just that if you want it.

So before we look at how, let's look at what an IDE is (or could be).

A typical IDE, if we talk of programs such as MS Visual Studio®, basically consists of the following things:

- An editor with automatic indentation, syntax coloring, and autocompletion
- An integrated compiler that makes it possible to jump directly to compile errors in the code
- An integrated debugger that makes it possible to step through the code
- A file explorer such that you can look through the files to add to the project
- A project browser to look through the files included in the project
- A tag browser to look through the tags (definitions, functions, methods, classes)
- An easy way to jump between files, definitions, and so on
- Maybe integration with some version / revision control system

So are all of these things, at all, possible in Vim? Now, let's go through all of the items, one by one, and see how we can get that functionality in Vim.

The first item is obvious, as Vim is an editor it does just that.

The second item in the list is the integration with a compiler. Vim is often used for programming, so it is built with support for compiler integration. For most common programming languages, the settings for compiler integration in Vim are already set. But if they are not, you can learn more about how to set up this feature in:

```
:help compiler
```

This functionality can be linked to a so-called quickfix list, which makes it easy to jump from a compile error to the place in the code where the actual error exists. You can then jump back and forth between the errors, correct them and then compile once again.

To learn more about quickfix lists, look in the help system under:

```
:help quickfix
```

The next item is an integrated debugger. This feature is, unlike the previous ones, not standard in Vim. There are, however, several different scripts that make the integration of debuggers in Vim easy. If you are using Linux, there is a script available called VimDebug. This script makes it possible to integrate gdb (C / C++ debugger), jdb (Java debugger), pdb (Python debugger), and the Perl debugger. You can find the latest version of this script at `http://www.vim.org/scripts/script.php?script_id=663`.

An alternative and more fully-featured debugger integration is called Clewn. This system integrates the gdb debugger with Vim and lets you use all of the functionality that the debugger would normally have. It even supports remote debugging if you want to debug an external system, without leaving your own system. You can find Clewn with instructions about installation and usage at `http://clewn.sourceforge.net`.

The next item is the file explorer. Vim comes with its own file explorer that makes it possible to browse directories and files on your system. However, a script has been constructed that makes the file browser even more compatible with an IDE-like setup. The script is called VtreeExplorer, and this makes it possible not only to browse the files, but also to see the contents of directories as a tree, which you can fold and unfold. This makes it very fast to navigate. You can find the script and information about how to use it here: `http://vim.sourceforge.net/scripts/script.php?script_id=184`.

Let's move on to the project manager part of the IDE. This component should make it possible to combine files into a project such that when you open a project, all the files in that particular project are also opened. If you are using Gvim, the script ProjMgr is a good choice when it comes to managing projects in Vim. It creates a menu item that holds lists of the available projects and the possibility to create new projects. You can find the script here: `http://vim.sourceforge.net/scripts/script.php?script_id=279`.

A version for normal console Vim is also available and can be found here: `http://www.vim.org/scripts/script.php?script_id=69`.

When it comes to browsing tags, it can be done in two variations. You can perform completion of tags and function names, among others, and then browse through the possibilities, or you can have a window that shows all of the available tags. To create such a window, I will recommend the script called TagList. This script supports all of the programming languages that the Ctags program (which it is also dependent on) supports. It shows a window with a nice list of all definitions, functions, methods, and classes, among others, and you can easily browse it and jump to the declaration of the tag. You can find the script and information about how to install it at `http://vim-taglist.sourceforge.net`.

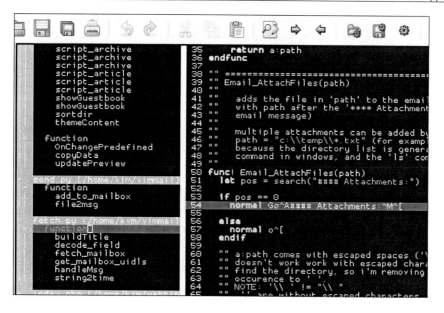

When it comes to moving around in the Vim editor window itself, Vim already has the shortcuts gf and gd, which take you to the file or declaration of the tag under the cursor. This makes it very fast to jump around in the files.

Finally, there is the integration with version / revision control systems such as CVS, SVN, and Perforce. As with all the other functionality that you need to construct a Vim IDE, this integration is of course also available via scripts. I would recommend the following scripts for the mentioned systems:

- CVS and SVN, which are located at `http://vim.sourceforge.net/scripts/script.php?script_id=90`

- Perforce, which is located at `http://vim.sourceforge.net/scripts/script.php?script_id=240`

So we have all the parts to complete our Vim IDE, and all we have to do now is put all the parts together and integrate them. If you don't want to go through this task, then some other Vim users have already done the job for you. An example is the **Vim JDE (Just a Development Environment)**, which integrates many of the mentioned scripts and combines them into a feature-rich IDE for Java, C, and C++ developers. You can find JDE and how to install it here:

`http://www.vim.org/scripts/script.php?script_id=1213.`

Another possibility is to follow one of the Vim tips on the Vim online community site where you can find tips that tell you how to set up the different scripts in order to integrate them. An example of such a tip is located at `http://www.vim.org/tips/tip.php?tip_id=1439`.

Mail program

Vim has for many years been able to be integrated in different programs and among those have been some mail clients—most notable is the open source mail client, Mutt.

For some Vim users, however, this was not enough, and they started to implement entire e-mail clients in Vim script—including support for sending, fetching, and organizing mail directly from within Vim.

 You can find the latest version of the free open source mail client Mutt here: `http://www.mutt.org/`.

In 2004, Suresh Govindachar created what he called **The Mail Suite (TMS)** for Vim. It was a mail client implemented partly in Vim script and partly in Perl script (embedded in Vim script). TMS has all you need in order to work with e-mails, and it even makes it possible to use all the features of Vim at the same time.

You can find The Mail Suite and instructions about installation and usage at `http://www.vim.org/scripts/script.php?script_id=1052`.

Another person who decided to implement an e-mail client in Vim was David Elentok. In 2005, he started creating an e-mail client for Vim by using a single Vim script and two Python scripts. The script is still in development, but already offers many of the main features you would want from an e-mail client.

You can find Mr. Elentok's scripts at the following address: `http://www.ee.bgu.ac.il/~elentok/files/vim/vim-mail/`.

Here, you can also find installation instructions and follow the development.

Chat with Vim

These days we almost never find a computer without some sort of chat application installed in it. It has, however, not always been like that. Back in the late 1980s, the concept of chatting on the Internet was limited to the Bulletin boards on some BBSs, but in 1988 the Finish guy Jarkko Oikarinen implemented a client-server chat solution he called **Internet Relay Chat (IRC)**. During the next decade, IRC became very popular and more and more people joined the chat networks every day. The concept was simple. Get an IRC client, let it connect to an IRC network server, join a chat channel about your favorite subject, and chat with people there.

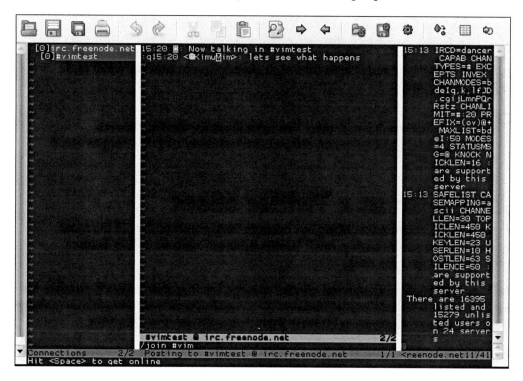

Many IRC clients exist, and in 2004, the Japanese Vim user Madoka Machitani started implementing an IRC client in Vim. He called the client VimIRC and what he constructed was a very feature-rich client that supports chatting in multiple channels on multiple networks. You can even use your normal Vim commands such as I, /, and ?, among others.

There is, however, a small problem when chatting from within Vim (besides the fact that it takes time from your actual project). In order for the chat to stay online, it has to create a loop that keeps updating everything. When you move to another buffer that has nothing to do with the IRC client, this loop is stopped and you are eventually disconnected from the network. So the trick to get this chat client working optimally is to start it in a Gvim or Vim of its own. This can be done directly on the command line with:

```
gvim -i NONE -i .vimircrc  -c VimIRC
```

Here `.vimircrc` is the path to a Vim configuration file with VimIRC-specific settings.

You can find the latest version of the VimIRC script at this address: `http://www.vim.org/scripts/script.php?script_id=931`.

Look at the top of the script for a thorough description of how to install and configure the script.

 You can chat with other Vim users if you use the IRC network `irc.freenode.net` and join the channel called **#vim**. See you there!

Using Vim as a Twitter client

In recent years, social networking has become very popular. One of the most popular platforms for sharing small "status updates" with friends is Twitter (`http://www.twitter.com`).

The Vim user Po Shan Cheah has created a script for Vim that makes it possible for you to read your friends' status updates. You can also post your own status updates and send privates messages to Twitter friends directly from within Vim.

The script is called TwitVim and can be found at the Vim script repository, which is located at `http://www.vim.org/scripts/script.php?script_id=2204`.

The script output is very simple and basically lists the last status updates from your friends on request. An example can be seen in the following picture:

```
User timeline*
————————*
kimschulz: @digsby: whats up with this error when posting to FB: Error posting comment.^@4: A
plication request limit reached |01:19  Jan 07, 2010|
kimschulz: Psystar Switches to Linux, Temporarily Halts Sales of Rebel EFI http://bit.ly/409Y
Z ( |10:45  Dec 29, 2009|
kimschulz: Så fik jeg også tid til at prøve @Dropbox. Ganske smart til fildeling og sync med
omputere. 2GB gratis plads! http://tinyurl.com/yjob8vc |11:31  Dec 22, 2009|
kimschulz: just installed handwriting hotfix for my @htc diamond2 but no handwriting is avail
ble....oh well may it does not work on danish wm6.5rom |11:12  Dec 18, 2009|
kimschulz: RT @pocketnowTweets: Nexus One Makes a Video Debut http://tinyurl.com/ydack9h |12:
2  Dec 16, 2009|
```

TwitVim uses the command-line program **cURL** (`http://curl.haxx.se/`) to fetch the information from Twitter. So, in order to use the script, you will have to install cURL on your computer.

 You can visit `http://www.twitter.com` for more information on Twitter and to sign up for an account for free.

B
Vim Configuration Alternatives

In Chapter 2, we looked at the main configurations files that Vim uses, and throughout the rest of the book, things were added to the `vimrc` configuration files. In the end, you might have a `vimrc` file full of settings mixed up in one big mess, making it hard to find things in the file.

In this appendix, we take a look at some ideas as to how to keep your `vimrc` file clean and well organized. The recipes range from simple tips to entire configurations systems.

Finally, we will take a look at how it is possible to use the same `vimrc` file on many different computers, simply by storing a copy of it online.

Tips for keeping your vimrc file clean

Your `vimrc` file is the heart of your personal Vim setup. Without this file, you are bound to have the same setup as the rest of the system. This is also the main reason for keeping this file clean and up-to-date, such that you always know what it contains, and where to find things in the file. It seems like a weird claim that you might not be able to find something in the file. I have, however, found myself in a situation where I had a `vimrc` file with more than 2000 lines. Then, I realized that I had to clean up my file in order to get in a state where I could again find things in it. Hence, here are some tips on how you can keep your `vimrc` file clean and organized:

1. **Always have Vim in nocompatible mode**

   This tip might not make your `vimrc` file any cleaner—at least not directly. It is, however, a very important tip. Having Vim in nocompatible mode, opens up a lot of features in Vim that other tips and scripts might take advantage of. So the first tip is to always have the following at the beginning of your `vimrc` file: `set nocompatible`.

2. **Use comments**

   At some point, we all have come across a tip about changing something in Vim, and then just added it to our `vimrc` file. Later, when we return to our `vimrc` file to modify it or perform a cleanup, we suddenly can't remember what that piece of Vim script did and why we added it. We don't even remember from where we got it. So instead of getting into this problem of not knowing what things do, just add comments to the things you add. What should you write? I would recommend that you write what it does (description), where you got it from (source), and who originally authored it (author). With this information, it is more likely that you can trace back to where you got it from, and in this way you make it possible to decide whether or not to keep the code. Comments are inserted by adding a " (double quote) in front of the comment like: `"This is a comment.`

3. **Group data**

   Often scripts need some extra settings or maybe you want to perform some extra key bindings (maps) for some functionality in the scripts. To make it clear what belongs together, it is a good idea to group the data. You can group it according to many different things, but I would recommend the following (ordered from the beginning of the file and downwards):

   - General system-wide setup
   - Key mappings for your own macros
   - Script-specific settings ordered per script
   - "Playground" with all of the script snippets and macros you find and test

4. **Use multiple files**

   Sometimes your `vimrc` file becomes really large, and no matter what you do the file is still cluttered. In that case, it might be better to split it into multiple files. To do so, you simply copy the parts you like (for example, the mapping group described in the previous tip) to a file with a descriptive name, and replace it in your `vimrc` file with a line that sources that particular file. In the case of the key mappings, the file could be called `mappings.vim`, and in your `vimrc` file you would then have, for example, `source $HOME/.vim/mappings.vim`.

5. **Use other files for tests**

   Previously, when I wanted to test some new piece of Vim script, macro, or mapping, I would just add it to the end of my `vimrc` file. Mostly, however, I forgot to remove it, and over time my `vimrc` file got filled with my test code. Instead of doing what I did, you should instead have an alternative file to add your code tests, and then simply source it to get the functionality into Vim. If you like the functionality, then you move the code to the right place in your `vimrc` file (or other settings file) and if not, simply delete the file.

6. **Use specific files for different operating systems / computers**

   If you, like I, have multiple computers that you use Vim on, you might experience that some `vimrc` configurations do not apply to all of the computers. This could be if the settings are operating system specific or if one computer, for example, has a small screen while the others might have bigger screens. In those cases, you can split out the system-specific settings / configurations into different files. This way you can have all of your generic configurations in a file you copy out on all systems and then have a system-specific file on each system that you just keep where it is needed.

If you follow these tips, you should hopefully be able to keep your `vimrc` file on a clean level, such that you always know where to change the settings for a certain task.

A vimrc setup system

When you use Vim, you will normally have to open up a configuration file in order to change the settings permanently. You can change all of them from within Vim, but after closing Vim, all of the settings are lost again.

But what if you had a system in Vim such that you could go into a settings menu, and the changes you made there were permanent for the system (until you change them again!)? This is actually possible with a little help from some Vim scripts created by Jos van RisWick.

By using his script, and creating your `vimrc` file using his special syntax, you can make it possible not only to make local changes permanent, but also to change the values in an easy-to-use settings wizard.

This is achieved by using the comments surrounding the setting as a placeholder for the information you are shown in the setup wizard. As I find this system both very smart and very different from what we normally use in Vim, I will give a short introduction to show how you use it.

So let's start by getting the parts we need in order to use this setup system.

The main script and all function scripts it relies on can be found at the following address: `http://www.vim.org/scripts/script.php?script_id=1894`.

The package contains the following scripts:

- `setup.vim`: The main script
- `array.vim`: Helper functions to work with string arrays
- `arrayg.vim`: Helper functions to work with string arrays (global)
- `strfun.vim`: Helper function to manipulate strings
- `tableaf.vim`: Script used to display tab leafs in the setup system

To install, you need to go into your VIMHOME and unpack the ZIP file. This will add all of the files to the `plugin/` folder.

Now you are ready to modify your `vimrc` file, but before you do that I urge you to make a copy of your existing `vimrc` file—just in case you don't like the setup system after all.

Before we start adding settings to our `vimrc` file (or other settings files), let's take a look at the syntax for using the setup system. As mentioned earlier, the trick is to use the comments surrounding the setting. Such a comment needs to have a very distinct syntax in order for the script to know what to do with it. The basic syntax is as follows: `"|ID|tabname|text|command|extra|val1|val2|val3|`.

Let's split it up into parts:

Part	Description
"	Begin comment.
ID	An identifier which the script can use to distinguish the different groups of settings. When the script is started, you tell it which group of settings it should work on.
tabname	Name of the tab (called leaf in the script) to add the setting to.
text	Text to show in relation to the setting.
command	The actual command to execute to set the setting. An example could be `set textwidth=` where the actual value is removed.

Part	Description
`extra`	If the command was, for example, a map, then the variable part is what keys to map and not the command. In that case, you would also want to be able to set what command to map the keys to. This is what you add in the extra field. If you don't need it, simply leave it out (like | |).
`val1-val3`	These are the default values you can use as arguments for the command. When in the setup system, you can cycle through the different values by using tab the key.

Now we have the basic syntax, so let's take an example of how this could look like:

```
"|SETTINGS|Layout|Set the text width|set tw=||50|70|90|
set tw=60
"|SETTINGS|Layout|Show a ruler?|let &ruler=||0|1|
let &ruler=1
```

This example shows two typical ways of setting up Vim—setting an option with `set`, and setting an option with `let`. By using `&` before the variable name, you tell Vim that the right-hand side of the equal sign is an expression that it should evaluate before setting it. This also means that if the type of the result of the expression is not the right one for the option, it will be converted automatically. The line below the comment is the actual setting as you want it per default.

If you simply want to add a comment in one of the tabs, you can do so by using a `%` symbol instead of the command, as follows:

```
"|SETTINGS|Layout|Here you will find layout settings|%|
```

You can also use this to add empty lines as spacers by replacing the text with a whitespace.

Now that you know how to create your settings you need to set up the script itself.

This is done in the script file `setup.vim` and can be found by simply searching for `HERE2` in the `setup.vim` file. The second time you hit the search word you are in the right place (the first one is in the introduction comments). Here, you will find the following settings:

```
" Import settings from these files HERE:
let setup_files=Arr("settings.vim","mappings.vim","scripts.vim")
let setup_group="SETTINGS"
```

The first setting, `setup_files`, is an array containing a list of the name of the files you have your settings in. In the previous example, the files `settings.vim`, `mappings.vim`, and `scripts.vim` are used.

The second setting tells the script which ID (as previously described) to use in this current setup. Here, we use SETTINGS, which means that all settings with a comment line above that starts with |SETTINGS| will be used.

Now you are almost ready and set to use the setup wizard, but you just need to change one more setting in the `setup.vim` file.

Because we have the settings split into several files, we need to make Vim aware of their existence. Therefore, we set the `vimrc` file to include (called "to source" in Vim) the different settings files. Because of this we also need Vim to reload our `vimrc` file, in order to load the new changes, and for this, we have a special setting in the file.

Search for HERE1 in the `setup.vim` file and once again go to the second hit from the top of the file. Here you will find a line where the script sources some file:

```
autocmd bufleave _setup source ~/.vimrc
```

This is an auto-command which is executed when you leave the setup wizard. You need to set it to source your `vimrc` file (or alternatively all of your external setting files), such that Vim will use the new settings.

Now you are all set up and it is time to learn how to start and navigate the Vim setup wizard. To start the setup wizard, you go into normal mode and press s. The cursor is placed on the first setting on the first tab in the settings editor. A number of key maps are now available for you to navigate and use the settings wizard.

You can see the different keyboard shortcuts in the following list:

Keyboard shortcuts	Description
r or R	Enter replace mode to change a setting
s	Save changes and quit the editor
q	Quit without saving the changes
<space>	Cycle through the tab leaves
j	Move to next setting on the current tab leaf
k	Move to previous setting on the current tag leaf
<tab>	Show alternative values for the selected setting
<cr>	Accept change on current line
<esc>	Redraw current tab leaf (normal mode)
<esc>	Discard change (insert / replace mode)

And that is really all you need in order to have an easy-to-use setup wizard built into Vim. So in the following screenshot, let's take a look at how the final result could look like in Vim:

Storing vimrc online

If you use Vim on many different computers, it is often annoying that you have to set up each Vim editor as you like it, or have to live with the many different setups.

These days where nearly all computers are connected to the Internet, an obvious solution to accommodate this problem is to store a copy of your `vimrc` file online. We already know that Vim can fetch and edit files from online sources such as web and FTP servers, but when you need to fetch and read a `vimrc` file instead for just reading your normal `vimrc` file, you will hit some problems. Normally, when Vim needs to read files on the net, it will use its `netrw` plugin. However, when Vim is reading the `vimrc` file it has not yet loaded the plugins, and hence cannot read the online version of the `vimrc` file.

This is, however, a problem we can get around with a bit of scripting, so let's take a look at how we can do this:

```
function! GetNetVimrc(vimrc_url)
    source $VIMRUNTIME/plugin/netrwPlugin.vim
    Nread a:vimrc_url
    let tmpfile = tempname()
    save! tmpfile
    source tmpfile
    delete(tmpfile)
    enew
endfunction
```

All of the functionality is combined in the GetNetVimrc function. This function takes a URL to where your vimrc file is stored online. The function starts by sourcing the netrw plugin, such that Vim gets access to the net read and write functions. Next, it uses the Nread function to read the vimrc file (given by the argument) from the net into the current buffer. The content of the buffer, which is actually the vimrc read from the net, is now written to a temporary file, which is then sourced to load the settings. Finally, the temporary file is deleted and a new clean buffer is opened.

So what do you actually have to do to get this to work?

First of all you will have to store your vimrc file online, somewhere where it is accessible. Besides this you will have to add the previous function to the vimrc file on all of the computers where you want to use your online vimrc version.

To actually activate the function, you could call it manually as:

```
:call GetNetVimrc("http://www.domain.com/myvimrc")
```

You can also simply add the previous line to all the vimrc files where you added the function.

Now Vim will act the same way on all computers you use, and if you update your online vimrc file, the changes will also be available on all of the other computers the next time you use Vim there.

Remember that you can change your online vimrc file directly from within Vim. Simply use the Nread and Nwrite functions to read and write the file.

Index

D

debugger commands
about 187
cont 187
finish 187
interrupt 187
next 187
quit 187
step 187
debugging
Vim scripts 186-188
drop registers 102

E

editor area, Vim
abbreviations, using 46-48
key bindings, modifying 49, 51
line numbers, adding 39
personalizing 37
spell check 40-42
tooltips, adding 43-46
editor area, Vimvisual cursor, adding 37, 38
Elvis
about 10
features 10
Emacs editor 13
expression register 103
exrc file 19
external formatting tools
about 136
Berkeley Par 137
Indent 136
Tidy 138
using 136
external interpreters
using in Vim scripting 194

F

file explorer 208
file navigation
about 54
context-aware navigation 54
long lines, navigating 59
File-Type plugins group 148
fold

about 107
diff, using to track changes 114
simple text file outlining 110, 111
types 107
using 107-109
vimdiff, using to track changes 111
foldclosed() function 45
fonts, Vim
changing 20
for loop 164, 165
formatexpr 123
formatting, Vim
code, formatting 129
external formatting tools, using 136
text, formatting 121
functions
creating 168-170
variable argument list 170-172

G

Game of Life 202
get function 163
Global plugins group 148
guitablabel property 36
gvimrc file 19

H

hacker 15
hacking 15
hasmapto() 178
helpgrep command 67
hidden markers
about 71
marks, using 71

I

IDE 208
indentexpr 132
Indent, external formatting tools 136
integrated compiler 207
integrated debugger 207
interpreter 15
Ispell 40

J

text, formatting
  about 121
  headlines, marking 125, 126
  lists, creating 127-129
  text, aligning 124
  text, putting into paragraphs 122, 123
The Mail Suite (TMS) 210
Tic-Tac-Toe 204
Tidy, external formatting tools 138
TwitVim 212

U

undo branching
  about 98
  using 103-106
unnamed register 100

V

variables
  about 153
  dictionary 153
  funcref 153
  list 153
  number 153
  string 153
v:folddashes variable 109
v:foldend variable 109
v:foldstart variable 109
vi 9
vi compatibility 14, 15
Vile
  about 13
  features 13
Vim
  about 7, 11
  advanced formatting 121
  autocompletion 84
  charityware license 15
  color scheme, changing 21
  command line buffer 26
  configuration files 18
  download link 8
  editor area, personalizing 37
  extensibility 141
  features 12
  fonts, changing 20

  hidden markers 71
  mail program 210
  marks, adding 68
  matching 22
  menu, adding 29-32
  menu, toggling 28, 29
  personal highlighting 22, 23
  personalizing 17
  scripting tips 182
  script structure 175
  search 63
  status line 26
  syntax-color schemes 141
  tabs, modifying 33-37
  toolbar icons, adding 32, 33
  toolbar, toggling 28, 29
  using, as Twitter client 212
  visible markers 68-70
Vimballs
  creating 190
vimdiff
  about 112
  navigation 113
  using, to track changes 111
vimdiff session 112
Vim documentation 191, 193
Vim editor. See Vim
Vim games
  about 201
  Game of Life 202
  Mines 204
  Nibbles 202
  Rubik's cube 203
  Sokoban 205
  Tetris 206
  Tic-Tac-Toe 204
VimIRC 211, 212
vimrc file
  about 18, 19
  cleaning, tips 215
  online storing 221
vimrc file, cleaning tips
  comments, using 216
  data, grouping 216
  multiple files, using 216
  Vim, using in nocompatible mode 216
vimrc setup system 217, 219

Thank you for buying
Hacking Vim 7.2

About Packt Publishing

Packt, pronounced 'packed', published its first book "*Mastering phpMyAdmin for Effective MySQL Management*" in April 2004 and subsequently continued to specialize in publishing highly focused books on specific technologies and solutions.

Our books and publications share the experiences of your fellow IT professionals in adapting and customizing today's systems, applications, and frameworks. Our solution based books give you the knowledge and power to customize the software and technologies you're using to get the job done. Packt books are more specific and less general than the IT books you have seen in the past. Our unique business model allows us to bring you more focused information, giving you more of what you need to know, and less of what you don't.

Packt is a modern, yet unique publishing company, which focuses on producing quality, cutting-edge books for communities of developers, administrators, and newbies alike. For more information, please visit our website: www.packtpub.com.

About Packt Open Source

In 2010, Packt launched two new brands, Packt Open Source and Packt Enterprise, in order to continue its focus on specialization. This book is part of the Packt Open Source brand, home to books published on software built around Open Source licences, and offering information to anybody from advanced developers to budding web designers. The Open Source brand also runs Packt's Open Source Royalty Scheme, by which Packt gives a royalty to each Open Source project about whose software a book is sold.

Writing for Packt

We welcome all inquiries from people who are interested in authoring. Book proposals should be sent to author@packtpub.com. If your book idea is still at an early stage and you would like to discuss it first before writing a formal book proposal, contact us; one of our commissioning editors will get in touch with you.

We're not just looking for published authors; if you have strong technical skills but no writing experience, our experienced editors can help you develop a writing career, or simply get some additional reward for your expertise.

open source
community experience distilled

PUBLISHING

C# 2008 and 2005 Threaded Programming: Beginner's Guide

ISBN: 978-1-847197-10-8   Paperback: 416 pages

Exploit the power of multiple processors for faster, more responsive software.

1. Develop applications that run several tasks simultaneously to achieve greater performance, scalability, and responsiveness in your applications

2. Build and run well-designed and scalable applications with C# parallel programming.

3. In-depth practical approach to help you become better and faster at managing different processes and threads

GDI+ Application Custom Controls with Visual C# 2005

ISBN: 978-1-904811-60-2   Paperback: 276 pages

A fast-paced example-driven tutorial to building custom controls using Visual C# 2005 Express Edition and .NET 2.0

1. Learn about custom controls and the GDI+

2. Walks through great examples like PieChart control

3. Customize and develop your own controls

Please check **www.PacktPub.com** for information on our titles

LaVergne, TN USA
24 October 2010

202031LV00003B/146/P